THE PERUVIAN PUZZLE

A Twentieth Century Fund Paper

THE PERUVIAN PUZZLE

BY FELIPE ORTIZ de ZEVALLOS

Priority Press Publications/New York/1989

The Twentieth Century Fund is a research foundation undertaking timely analyses of economic, political, and social issues. Not-for-profit and nonpartisan, the Fund was founded in 1919 and endowed by Edward A. Filene.

Library of Congress Cataloging-in-Publication Data
Ortiz de Zevallos M., Felipe.
The Peruvian puzzle.

"A Twentieth Century Fund paper"
1. Debts, External—Peru. 2. Peru—Economic conditions. 3. Peru—Politics and government.
4. Peru—Economic conditions—1968- .
5. Peru—Politics and government—1980- . I. Title.
HJ8604.O78 1988 336.3'4'0985 88-32496
ISBN 0-87078-233-9
ISBN 0-87078-232-0 (pbk.)

Manufactured in the United States of America.

Foreword

In 1985, when Alan Garcia Perez was sworn in as president, expectations ran high in Peru. His youth—he was only thirty-six—and his charisma held out the promise of a leader capable of extricating the nation from its economic and political crises. Further enhancing his appeal was his promise not to succumb to the demands of Peru's creditors: his vow that Peru would pay no more than 10 percent of its export earnings to meet debt-service obligations on some $14 billion of international debts. Nearly five years later—besieged by economic depression, hyperinflation, and terrorist violence—Peru's future looks grim and its debt burden remains crushing.

From the inception of the Fund's series of papers on the international debt crisis, we have sought to examine the issues within a broad framework, but with a concentration on Latin American debt. In our two papers on Mexico, *The Mexican Time Bomb,* by Norman Bailey and Richard Cohen, and *A Mexican Response,* by Luis Rubio F. and Francisco Gil-Diaz, we supported opposing views of the implications of the crisis for the stability of the government—more specifically for the ruling PRI—as well as for economic development. Marcilio Marques Moreira's assessment of his country's dilemma in *The Brazilian Quandary* was shaped by his strong and controversial view that money borrowed had benefited the Brazilian economy. In *The Costa Rican Laboratory,* Sol Sanders probed the consequences of debt for that model democracy.

But our examination of Latin America's problems would not have been complete without an analysis of Peru. Thus, the Fund invited Felipe Ortiz de Zevallos, an able economist with a passionate commitment to his country, to trace the history of Peru's problems and to chart a new course of action. In doing so he spares none of the parties—the Peruvian government must get its house in order, the U.S. government must be willing to consider a write-down of at least some debt, the commercial banks must at the very least accept caps on interest rates, and the IMF and World Bank must allow representatives of Third World governments to play a more meaningful role in determining their future. These recommendations—because of their candor—bear heeding. We are grateful to Ortiz de Zevallos for them.

Marcia Bystryn, ACTING DIRECTOR
The Twentieth Century Fund
January 1989

Contents

Most North Americans have a picture, based on news headlines and *New Yorker* cartoons, of a Latin America governed by comical, mustachioed men on horseback who gallop in and out of the presidential palace with monotonous regularity. Our other image is of poor but happy peasants with big *sombreros* either taking *siestas* under the palm trees or dancing gaily in the streets. Latin America is no longer comic opera or the stuff of cartoons. Instead, politics and the clash of social forces have become deadly serious, with the stakes high and the outcome still uncertain.

—Howard J. Wiarda and Harvey F. Kline,
Latin American Politics and Development (Westview Press, 1985).

Peru is an example of a country in need of debt relief. The economy has been in a state of collapse due to the combined pressures of falling export prices, fifteen years of poor economic management, and the heavy weight of debt servicing. Per capita GNP has declined by 15 percent since 1980, and real wages have fallen by an incredible 40 percent. The social fabric is crumbling. Murder, kidnapping, and terrorism are the daily fare of Lima. Drug trafficking provides one of the few profitable activities in a collapsing economy. However, when President Alan Garcia Perez told the United Nations last year that his country faced the choice of debt or democracy, and that therefore he would unilaterally restrict debt servicing payments, his *cri de coeur* was received as an affront to the banks, and the international financial community has united in opposition to his plea for debt relief.

—Jeffrey D. Sachs, "A New Approach to Managing the Debt Crisis,"
Columbia Journal of World Business, Fall 1986

Peru has recently been declared ineligible for further International Monetary Fund assistance (and hence probably for all external credit) because of its refusal to make more than token interest payments to the IMF and other creditors. Peru's economy is in particularly difficult straits; per capita income is now less than 20 years ago. The country's democratic institutions are under siege, not only from economic reversals, but also from a fierce guerrilla insurgency and widespread drug trafficking. Relations between Peru's civilian authorities and its armed forces are sensitive and unpredictable.

Although Peru is in violation of IMF rules, the international community should not turn its back on that troubled country. Peru needs international assistance to confront its financial difficulties and to strengthen its democratic institutions. Precisely because Peru is a democracy, it deserves to be treated with consideration and respect. It would be wrong to use Peru as a lesson to deprive the country of the resources it requires to overcome its massive economic problems.

—Sol M. Linowitz, *Miami Herald,* December 21, 1986.

1 / History Repeats Itself

Introduction

In 1982, just as Mexico was creating an international uproar by announcing it was suspending payment of its debt service, the Peruvian government asked Merrill Lynch, Pierce, Fenner & Smith, Inc. to help prepare a short booklet entitled "Peru: Background Information" as part of what turned out to be a very successful campaign to get new loans.

That elegant and expensive booklet prepared by Peru's financial advisers proclaimed:

> The present government has made significant progress in accomplishing its major goals . . . and is fostering an environment conducive to the country's long-term political, economic and social development.[1]

Had those who succumbed to its rhetoric noticed, a short, telltale footnote stated that the financial advisers were not responsible for the accuracy or completeness of the information in the booklet. The footnote should have alerted investors to the fact that there was a problem, and a little research would have told them that the Peruvian government had a history of defaulting on its external commitments almost every fifty years: in 1825, 1876, 1931.

And, sad to say, history did repeat itself. As a result of its public campaign effort, Peru's public external debt rose by 11 percent in 1982 while its GDP only rose by 0.9 percent. Then, in 1983 Peru suffered its worst year in this century due to ecological disasters and initiated a "conciliatory" default.[2]

Not surprisingly, some hypothesized that both Peru and the international creditors involved committed basically the same mistakes in each of the crises. And there were similar situations in Peru each time. For example,

- There have been constant struggles between the numerous and very distinct economic and social groups in Peruvian society that result in dramatic policy shifts. Throughout its republican history, no one group has ever gained long-term leadership over the others, nor has a wide-ranging social accord ever been reached. As a result, there have been recurrent internal conflicts on decisions regarding budgetary allocations and the prices of consumer goods, and this has had particularly dramatic effects in a country that imports a significant amount of food.
- There has been a tendency to expect a steady stream of income from what are essentially natural resource windfalls; such was the case with guano, nitrates, copper, fishmeal, oil, and gas. Furthermore, tax exemptions and evasion have been rampant.
- There have been erratic shifts in exchange rate policies. Uncertainty about terms of trade has been the rule rather than the exception because the prices for Peruvian exports have always tended to remain highly volatile while import prices have moved steadily upward. Moreover, projections of future exports have normally been too optimistic. In addition, Peru—indeed most LDCs—lives almost constantly on the edge of its means, and has insufficient internal savings.
- Defense has historically been responsible for a significant part—perhaps, 25 percent—of imports, of budgetary expenditures, and of foreign indebtedness.
- Government bureaucracy and government subsidies have grown with every new administration. The budget is normally seen as a pork barrel for vested interests, and decisions about investment in new projects are based on political rather than economic criteria.
- The economy centers on borrowing whenever international credit is available, heavily mortgaging the future, particularly to foreign banks, which have been inconsistent regarding Peru's longer-term credit requirements. Sometimes the banks have pushed loans; at other times, when a growing portion of the budget was required to service the foreign debt and things became critical, banks changed tack abruptly, denying loans. The result, in an economy with a weak domestic capital market, has been that the government has turned to the printing press.

The development of the three earlier crises shows how little was learned from history.

The First Loans[3]

The first registered international debts of Peru in the London market (in 1822 and 1825) were entered into in order to finance the fight for independence from Spain. Jose de San Martin, an Argentinian general in command of the armies of Argentina and Chile, which had already gained independence, sailed to Peru to an enthusiastic welcome. On July 28, 1821, he declared the country independent. Spain resisted, and a three-year war was fought in which thousands of Peruvians were killed fighting both as royalists and republicans.

The first loan, to purchase ammunition and pay for troops, was for 1.2 million pounds sterling, to be paid back in thirty years at 6 percent per year interest and 2 percent in commissions. In spite of the fact that the loan was to a republic that was still fighting for its independence, English creditors managed to convince themselves that it was sound because Peru was a legendary producer of precious metals.

This loan was followed by one of 616,000 pounds sterling for payment of the first two years' interest on the first loan. (Peru's creditors were taking a path its future creditors would be eager to follow.) These loans were made during a period in which the economy almost collapsed as Peru became the battlefield for South American independence. The problem was compounded when, as 1825 drew to a close, international interest rates rose and world prices for raw material exports fell. Peru—as well as other Latin American countries—defaulted on its debt.

In the aftermath of the war for independence, Peru took much longer than most Latin American countries to develop a reasonably stable political system, in large part because the war did not bring to prominence Peruvian statesmen capable of leading the country. As a result, during the early years of the republic, all heads of state were military. Peru had at least fifteen constitutions in its first forty years as an independent country, but force remained the normal route to political power. Of the thirty-five presidents during this period, only four were indirectly elected according to constitutional procedures. There was not to be an elected civilian president until 1872.

The price of this political turmoil was a failure to develop a stable economic system, and this failure combined with another "natural resource" misunderstanding helped ensure the next crisis.

The Age of Guano

The independence debt hung over the nation until the 1840s, when a somewhat homely product—guano, or bird droppings—brought about an economic boom. Guano, a natural fertilizer with high nitrogen content—huge deposits were found on islands off the Peruvian coast—was unique until the advent of largely artificial substitutes, and it acquired a monopoly position in the world fertilizer market. According to an article that was published by *Fortune* in January 1938, guano gave Peru US$375 million ("more than all the mines of the Incas"[4]) during the Age of Guano, which lasted until 1875, when supplies were practically exhausted.

The first sale of guano to Europe had taken place in 1840, and its profitability coincided with growing political stability and economic recovery from the effects of the independence wars. Guano gradually became the basis for government deficit spending and foreign indebtedness as successive governments mortgaged future guano production to meet immediate needs and financed a system of railroads that were uneconomical and never completed. For a quarter of a century, Peru was one of the heaviest borrowers in European capital markets with guano as its chief collateral.

Then the European financial panic created by the collapse of the Vienna stock market in 1873 both affected Peru's ability to obtain new loans to cover deficits and lessened demand for its exports. Peru reached a point where the demands on the budget for debt repayment, railroad building, military expenditures, and corruption coincided with declining guano supplies and an unwillingness on the part of creditors to grant loans as advances on production. However, it was not until January 1, 1876, that the country fell officially into default. Income from guano exports totaled 2.8 million pounds sterling for that year, and debt payment was about the same. And again, Peru was not alone; during those years, Honduras, Costa Rica, the Dominican Republic, Spain, Turkey, and Egypt also defaulted.

The Road to the Next Default

This difficult period in Peru's history grew worse with the outbreak of the War of the Pacific with Chile (1879-1883). As a consequence of the war, Chile wrested from Peru the port of Arica and the coastal department of Tarapaca with its immense nitrate deposits, and for some years, it occupied a large portion of the country, including Lima, the capital city.

Politically, this defeat demonstrated the weakness of existing institutions and contributed to the emergence of Peru's only sustained period of limited liberal democracy (1895-1919). Economically, the war left the country bankrupt. To survive, Peru mortgaged many of its basic resources, becoming even more dependent on British interests. Peru's debts in sterling, accumulated as a result of the war, amounted to more than US$200 million; they were written off in 1889 by British interests in exchange for Peru's railroads and the Lake Titicaca steamship line, a large tract of jungle land, free use of major ports, and large quantities of guano. Years later, in his book *Inside Latin America,* John Gunther was to write:

> Peru is the classic regional example of a colonial economy. Natives control a certain amount of sugar production, as well as wool and cotton, but almost all the rest (oil, mining, textiles, railroads, shipping, communications, breweries, flour mills, electricity, banking) is owned by foreigners, a cause of disgust for many Peruvians.[5]

The period of limited democracy was marked by renovation, modernization, and innovation. The civilian rulers of the period also advanced the classic liberal precept of government as the facilitator of the private sector and fostered substantially increased government expenditures on communications, education, and health. Such improvements were financed by the rapid expansion of exports, by encouragement given to new foreign investment, particularly from the United States, and by new foreign loans granted once Peru's international credit was restored in 1907. For example, a loan was arranged in 1909 to increase the defense capacity of the country. There was also a loan for the city of Lima contracted in 1911 with a government guarantee. But due to world conditions, credit was not available from 1912 until after World War I.

Then, in 1919, with the election of President Augusto B. Leguia, a new borrowing process that was to last a decade began. This time the borrowing shifted increasingly toward U.S. resources, and the lion's share was used to cover even larger budget deficits. By 1927, for instance, more than half of fiscal revenues came from borrowing, especially borrowing abroad. Consequently, government debt—both internal and external—soared in this period. Economic conditions—in Peru and in the world—grew worse, and Leguia, who ruled through the "roaring twenties," was ousted by the military in 1930, after the 1929 crash that sent the world economy into a collapse.

Decades of deficit spending were only partially responsible for Peru's economic problems. U.S. Senate hearings on the matter in 1932 and 1933 revealed that New York bankers and the U.S. government had pushed loans on Peru in an "undignified scramble."[6] Thus, the blame for Peru's moratorium in 1931 can be laid on both doorsteps: a good part of the proceeds from these loans simply stayed in New York as service payments on earlier loans, another portion was invested in unprofitable ventures in public works around Lima.

Edwin W. Kemmerer, a professor at Cornell and Princeton, who led a U.S. technical mission to Peru after the coup, estimated that the external debt at the end of 1930 was US$123 million. Exports during that year were about US$80 million and dropped to US$60 million the following year. As a result of the economic problems facing the nation, Kemmerer himself was not totally against the selective default of 1931.

Into the Modern Period

Economic, political, and social developments in Peru in the modern era must be examined in the context of developments in the APRA (Alianza Popular Revolucionaria Americana) party. In 1924, Victor Raul Haya de la Torre, an exiled student leader who was to become the dominant figure in Peruvian politics in the twentieth century, founded APRA, which soon became a genuinely mass-based political organization with a fully articulated if not completely coherent ideology.

The 1930s and 1940s. From the beginning of the thirties, the traditionally dominant Peruvian groups, which never developed a comparable party, were forced to rely on the military to protect their economic and political interests from APRA, which was strong enough to win or determine the outcome of any open election. And until 1985, the military was strong enough to use various legal or illegal means of keeping APRA from ruling directly.

On the economic front, the 1931 moratorium dampened borrowing, which meant that exports became a major source of finance for imports. This change made domestic capital the major source of finance for state and industrial development, and no new foreign debt was contracted till the 1940s. Then, after World War II, and with a view to expanding investment in the Cerro de Pasco mines, the U.S. government began granting small loans to the Peruvian government. But it took until 1947—interestingly enough, on the initiative of Manuel Seoane, a prominent APRA leader and senator—for the Peruvian parliament to agree to start consolidating existing arrears. This debt was termed "the old debt," for purposes of amortization.

The president of Peru at that time was Jose Luis Bustamante y Rivero, a civilian elected in the free election of 1945; he was backed by the Frente

[Front] Democratico Nacional (FDN), a coalition that included APRA (the first time APRA had an official role in the government) as a leading partner. Inflation, which began to be a problem in the early forties due to subsidies and defense spending, surged during the Bustamante years. He entered office with great plans to develop the country and to improve the economic condition of the masses. However, in a time of increased inflationary demands, his government fixed the exchange rate, restricted access to foreign by means of import licenses, and granted different exchange rates to importers on the basis of certain social value judgments. These policies hurt the export sector and exacerbated the economic problems facing Peru.

Finally, toward the end of his regime, President Bustamante made attempts to stabilize the economy and partially reconcile his position with that of the export sector. His adjustment program of September 1948 received IMF approval—and marked Peru's first contact with that nascent organization. The FDN alliance, however, did not prove viable, and a month later, a right-wing military coup led by General Manuel Odria put an end to it.

Bustamante himself later wrote about the problems he had faced:

> Three principal adverse factors were operative during my regime: the scarcity of foodstuffs, monetary inflation and the deficiency of gold reserves (foreign exchange) to meet the demands of international trade. A fourth factor could be added to the list, namely the tremendous lack of prestige of our external credit.[7]

The 1950s. Liberal policies toward foreign investment and a rise in export prices caused by the Korean War dramatically improved the Peruvian economy during the early fifties. Creditworthiness was restored by paying outstanding arrears, and in February 1954, Peru signed the first standby arrangement ever devised by the IMF.[8] According to Thomas Scheetz,[9] this program, which first formally introduced conditionality and "close consultation," was groundbreaking. Every year for the next fifteen years, the Peruvian government was to sign another such agreement as additional insurance against possible balance of payments disequilibria. These IMF-supplied lines of credit were not drawn upon until 1958, when a crisis did force an adjustment program, which was the first ever to state the borrowing conditions in a letter of intent.

The fifties were also a period marked by mounting social tension. Dr. Manuel Prado, a clever urban oligarch, was elected president in 1956 with the support of APRA. In 1959, one of his ministers hired Arthur D. Little Inc. to prepare an analysis of Peru's economic development. Its report—*A Program for the Industrial and Regional Development of Peru*[10]—declared that the "national effort for economic development must be as quick and as sweeping as a mobilization for war."

The report, which clearly summarized the situation in Peru at the end of the fifties, went on to warn that

> political stability and long-range economic survival are seriously jeopardized by the population explosion, the subsistence standards of living of more than half of the population, and the concentration of wealth in the hands of a few. Unless the danger of this situation is recognized and resources are mobilized to meet the impending danger, vast numbers of Peruvians will not have the opportunity to earn a livelihood nor to survive in any state of decency.
>
> Traditional attitudes toward capital, labor and consumption are obstacles to increased investment in industry, serve to limit the size and growth of the markets, restrict labor mobility and productivity, and discourage public acceptance of locally made goods. These attitudes, if not modified, will seriously retard the rate of industrial development. Some examples of these views include: the traditional habit of investing capital in real estate and trade, rather than in productive industry; the preference for small family-size industrial holdings; preoccupation with the local market and a lack of thinking about export market possibilities, the low volume-high markup approach to trade; over-protection of industries from imported goods resulting often in poor quality and over-priced merchandise; a disinclination to promote competition among local industries, and labor policies which restrict production and overemphasize deferred social benefits.

2 / The Recent Crisis

The Past Twenty-five Years

In 1963, Fernando Belaunde Terry was elected president on a platform of nationalizing the International Petroleum Company, which belonged to Standard Oil of New Jersey, implementing an agrarian reform, and changing the taxation system. This populist platform won him the election but antagonized the U.S. government. The U.S. State Department responded by declaring official loans to Peru undesirable: Peru was not to receive Alliance for Progress funds nor loans from multilateral institutions. It was, for all practical purposes, blocked out of the offical lending market of the time.

But private sources were willing to lend Peru substantial amounts. In 1964, Peru contracted with a syndicate led by Manufacturers Hanover Trust, with the participation of Bankers Trust, First National City Bank (Citibank), and Continental Illinois, for a loan of US$40 million. A second significant private loan was signed in 1967 with the same syndicate at a cost equal to the first loan—1 3/4 percent over prime, one year's grace period, five years' payback. However, one year later, these debt obligations could not be met, and it became necessary to refinance them.* In October 1968, while the refinancing was being arranged, there was a coup d'etat that put into power a populist and nationalistic military government led by General Juan Velasco.

The underlying themes of Velasco's regime, which held power until 1975, included a commitment to change, national pride, social solidarity, an end of "dependency"; a worker-managed economy; and a "fully participatory social democracy which should be neither capitalistic nor communistic but humanistic." Peru then reestablished relations with Cuba

* Economic and financial management during President Fernando Belaunde Terry's first spell in power has been so well explained by Pedro-Pablo Kuczynski[1] that it obviates the need for further description here.

and the USSR. For example, when the U.S. government blocked arms sales to the Peruvian armed forces, the air force and the army bought from the Soviets; the navy, ideologically more conservative, turned instead to Italy, Germany, and Holland for the purchase of needed modern weaponry.

The economic results of General Velasco's regime have been described by Daniel Schydlowsky:

> Pursuing fairness in agriculture led to an agrarian reform in 1969 that broke up the large sugar and cotton estates and reduced the output of this major foreign exchange producing sector, thus aggravating the imbalance between foreign exchange production and foreign exchange usage. The "industrial community" legislation of 1970 had the same effect. It provided very strong incentives for the substitution of labor by capital, but the capital goods were largely imported so the import intensity of new industrial investment rose substantially. Moreover, the exchange controls of 1970, which accompanied the trade policy, made it very attractive to overinvoice machinery and to operate with imported inputs, also preferably overinvoiced, in order to expatriate assets the private sector feared would ultimately be confiscated in any case. Once Peru's development policies were set, the countdown to a collision between the demand for foreign exchange and its availability was under way.[2]

In its efforts to avoid, or at least postpone, this collision, the military regime continued the process of increasing indebtedness.

General Francisco Morales Bermudez, who replaced Velasco in 1975, later announced that there would be elections to put in place a civilian government in 1980. The elections restored Belaunde Terry to power. But regardless of the political changes, the cycle of foreign borrowing continued. Then, in 1984, as before in Peruvian history, the international financial markets closed their doors to Peru. Once that happened, it became obvious to all that the country was bankrupt, that loans had not been used productively, and that the country's capacity to pay depended, among other factors, on the international financial system.

The Development of the Current Debt

The development of the Peruvian external debt between 1970, when a letter of intent to the IMF was signed, and 1985, the year after the country began to default, can be divided into four periods (see Table 2.1).

The first period lasted from 1970 to 1973; in those years, the medium- and long-term public debt increased from US$986 million to US$1,508 million, despite the fact that the total foreign debt increased proportionately much less, from US$3,681 million to US$4,132 million. In these years, which were marked by political confrontation, Peru hardly received any loans from the United States Agency for International Development (USAID) or from the Export-Import Bank (EXIMBANK). It also received little aid from the World Bank and the Inter-American Development Bank (IDB), in which the U.S. influence is decisive: one loan in the case of the World Bank and nothing but reconstruction credits from IDB following a 1970 earthquake disaster.

In the next five-year period (1973-1978), Peru's medium- and long- term public debt practically quadrupled, owing principally to increasing fiscal deficits due to the expansion of the public sector. This took the total external debt from US$4,132 million in 1973 to US$9,324 million in 1978. This was aggravated by Peruvian military worries about the right-wing coup in Chile in 1973 and associated increases in defense spending.

Curiously enough, despite the Peruvian government's reformist rhetoric and the cooling off of U.S.-Peruvian relations till 1974, when Peru signed an agreement compensating for previous expropriations of U.S. interests, international banks proved amenable to satisfying the Peruvian government's finance requests. The result was that the combination of a price rise for exports and the inflow of capital managed to postpone the mo-

Table 2.1
Peruvian External Debt from 1970 to 1985 (US $ million)

	1970	*1973*	*1978*	*1980*	*1985*
External Debt					
Long Term	2,190	2,790	7,226	8,126	12,677
1. Public-Sector	986	1,508	5,886	6,753	11,335
Government and Agencies	945	1,491	5,135	6,043	10,510
Central Bank	41	17	751	710	825
2. Private Sector	1,204	1,201	1,340	1,373	1,342
Short-Term	1,491	1,423	2,098	1,469	1,117
Total External Debt	3,681	4,132	9,324	9,595	13,794
Annual Exports	1,034	1,112	1,972	3,916	2,978
Debt/Exports Ratio	3.6	3.7	4.7	2.4	4.6

Source: Central Bank

ment of explosion in the balance of payments. By the same token, when that explosion did come, it was more significant than it would have been earlier. (Some basic economic indicators of the Peruvian economy are shown in Appendix 1.)

From 1975 on, it was obvious that latent imbalances would grow out of control unless coherent adjustment and stabilization policies were adopted. The situation did in fact run wild, with prices—which rose 24 percent in 1975—leaping a further 45 percent in 1976.

Surprisingly, despite a grave external-sector crisis—the current account balance fell to -11.3 percent of GDP in 1975—international banks, with a glut of petrodollars, displayed a quite unprecedented willingness to lend Peru another US$400 million without IMF intervention. They opted, instead, for an agreement with the government on a less rigid stabilization policy than the one proposed by the IMF, which would be monitored by a "Steering Committee" composed of Bank of America, Chase Manhattan Bank, Manufacturers Hanover, Morgan Guaranty Trust, Wells Fargo Bank, and Citibank. The agreement called for a devaluation of the local currency by over 40 percent, increases in government-controlled prices, elimination of a large number of subsidies, and some minor budget cuts.

Upon the signing of the contract, the banks immediately disbursed US$200 million—without Peru applying the economic measures agreed upon. The remaining US$200 million was supposed to be disbursed when Peru complied with the terms of the agreement. The interest rate was to be LIBOR plus 2.25 percent, with 1.5 percent commission and a 5.5-year payback period, with two years' grace. The unusual circumstances of this loan have become the object of considerable study by experts, who frequently cite it as a prime case of private commercial banks' inability to devise and monitor a stabilization program in a debtor nation.

Why most of the banks involved were prepared to launch this kind of financial adventure without IMF backing is none too clear. One hypothesis is that the banks did not want to risk a possible default by Peru—at that time one of the most heavily indebted developing countries, particularly to private sources of finance—because unilateral nonpayment could have set off a chain reaction. Another possibility is that the banks were trying to boost General Morales's position as the new president of the military regime, since he had expressed willingness to comply with Peru's commitments to the international financial system. One New York banker involved in the negotiations made the point very succinctly: the "main reason" for the loan was "to perpetuate Morales Bermudez in power"[3] since the bankers considered this the best bet for getting their money back.

The banks' decision was not, however, unanimous. Some, like Bankers Trust and Continental Illinois, for instance, refused to take part in the syndicated loan, arguing that an operation of this kind would damage their reputations. And as social tensions grew, it became evident to the bankers that their new role was perceived as infringing on Peruvian sovereignty. In early 1977, having learned a bitter lesson, they passed the Peruvian hot potato to the IMF, but not before being severely burned by a secret arms deal between Peru and the USSR. (In November 1976, the military government while demanding financial support from Western banks was simultaneously buying a fully financed fleet of Soviet-armed planes.)

The IMF diagnosed Peru's problems in its usual textbook way: Peru had an overheated economy that needed to be cooled off quickly. The prescription involved a drastic reduction of government deficit and credit expansion. Of all Latin American countries affected by the debt crisis, Peru does seem to have suffered more than its fair share of rigid interventionism on the part of the Fund, not to mention insensitivity. (Turkey, in much the same position, received much more favorable treatment for political reasons.) Thomas Scheetz, who has made an extensive analysis of the role of the IMF in Peru during this period, concludes:

> The IMF's model makes for neither good theory nor good policy. Its assumptions are either incorrect or heavily value laden. . . . Because the disease is inadequately perceived, the cure can, at best, be a stopgap measure, and, at worst, lead to disaster. The social and development costs are not figured into the stabilization program. This most certainly reveals the IMF's value bias and at the same time undercuts its claim to present an objective, scientific approach to a country's financial problems that does not violate its sovereignty and political institutions.[4]

In addition, the resistance to reducing public expenditures and numerous shifts in economic policy in this period (from May 1977 until June 1978 there were four different finance ministers) created a chronic state of crisis from which the Peruvian economy still has not fully recovered.

The third stage in the development of Peru's debt goes from 1978 to 1980; in this period, a severe and coherent adjustment was designed by local authorities and applied with the support of the IMF. This adjustment did not succeed in bringing down inflation because of a sudden rise in export prices and the corresponding expansion of domestic liquidity. However, since Peru was able to repay some of its foreign debt during this period, its total debt only rose by US$270 million over these two years, and the ratio of external debt to annual exports fell from 4.7 to 2.4.

Unfortunately, increases in public spending during President Fernando Belaunde Terry's second administration (the fourth stage, 1980-1985) combined with unforeseeable natural disasters and an increasingly unfavorable external environment to once again widen fiscal and balance of payments gaps. By 1985, the debt-to-exports ratio was back again to 4.6. In addition, the second Belaunde administration was faced unexpectedly with the problem of growing violence associated with the terrorist activities of the radical political group known as the Shining Path (Sendero Luminoso).

Based in the isolated southern-central sierra province of Ayacucho and headed by Abimael Guzman-Camarada Gonzalo, a former professor from the local University of Huamanga—the Shining Path guerrillas call for a peasant-controlled republic created by revolution and based on the principles of Mao in order to create "a new society, without exploited nor exploiters, without oppressed nor oppressors, without classes, nor State, nor parties, nor democracy, nor arms, nor war."[5] During the past five years, over 10,000 people have died in the struggle, and, as a result, twelve provinces have been completely militarized.

None of these challenges and constraints absolves the Belaunde government from its economic policy failures. President Belaunde was always relatively disinterested in basic economic development principles, focusing instead on promoting long-term, large-scale public works in housing and roads. But his efforts in this direction were aided by the international institutions. In mid-1981, for example, the World Bank supported the government proposal of a US$11.5 billion, five-year public development program in a consultative group meeting in Paris.

Many bureaucrats at that time were apparently unconcerned by the fact that this investment program would catapult the public-sector deficit to almost 10 percent of GDP. These deficits were covered with new foreign borrowing. Most of the increase in the total debt in this period, from US$9,595 million in 1980 to US$13,794 million in 1985, corresponded to the rise in public-sector expenditures.

From 1980 on, the total external debt grew considerably more in Peru than in other Latin American countries. When export prices declined steadily in 1982, the currency collapsed and the reserves were all but depleted. Despite these ominous developments, neither the Fund nor the government were evidently prepared for the economic catastrophe that struck Peru in 1983. Global demand for the basic commodities, such as copper, that make up Peru's exports continued to slump. The damage caused by a series of natural disasters, especially widespread flooding, compounded the adverse effects of low commodity prices. Compounding the crisis, during the early months of that year Peru agreed to undertake a program with the IMF based on unrealistic economic projections made by that organization and accepted by the minister of economy and finance.

Following that agreement, massive injections of new money and reschedulings of principal were negotiated with the foreign banks, totaling US$1.6 billion—more than twice the amount requested by the government in the beginning of the year. But even this was not enough to compensate for the negative shocks the economy had suffered (exports earned US$500 million less than forecasted). As a result of all this, in 1983 Peru's gross domestic product declined by a catastrophic 12 percent, the government lost a third of its tax revenues, the debts of private companies rose to unsustainable levels, and inflation moved into triple digits.

Admittedly, the International Monetary Fund could not have predicted the natural disasters, but this does not explain the large gap between their projections, upon which the 1983 standby arrangement had been based, and what happened. As late as November 1983, the Fund was predicting "only" a 6 percent decline in gross domestic product—half the size of the decline that actually took place. Nor were negotiations helped by the attitude of some government officials, who were unwilling to face reality. Finally, under pressure from Peru's commerical creditors, with whom yet another rescheduling agreement had been awaiting approval since August, the IMF and the government assembled a new arrangement in early 1984. Like its predecessor, the 1984 standby agreement paid no more than lip service to the reforms required to produce greater output from the Peruvian economy.

And, like the preceding agreement, the 1984 version was based on hopelessly unrealistic projections—not only of economic trends, but also concerning the ability of a weak government to carry through draconian fiscal measures in the face of plummeting living standards, declining commodity prices (and hence lower tax revenues), and an intolerably large interest burden on external debt. Even a government operating in much more favorable economic and political circumstances would have had difficulties carrying out such a program.

It was, to say the least, careless of the Fund to approve commitments that the most superficial analysis would have shown to be unattainable. Not surprisingly, therefore, the life span of the 1984 standby agreement was short. By July, the government was again in need of cash—despite a 25 percent decline in real public-sector wages, a similar reduction in state investment, and a drastic lowering of food subsidies and military expenditures. The few months of pseudorespectability granted by the agreement, however, provided enough time for the rescheduling agreement with the commercial banks to be signed; and US$130 million worth of new money was added to Peru's already intolerable debt burden.

During the final year of the Belaunde government, the authorities pursued a policy of "we will do our best," maintaining dialogue with the Fund and remitting payments on an ad hoc basis to the commercial banks, when the monthly cash flow permitted such payments to be made. In addition, since 1985 the USSR had accepted payment in kind instead of rolling over its military debt, and those shipments of nontraditional exports provided for a mild reactivation of local industries.

The Lessons Learned

In short, over the past twenty-five years, Peru has endured many different kinds of governments with all kinds of economic policies. The main weakness of all of them has been the inability of policymakers to distinguish between problems that can be solved and conditions that are almost impossible to change. Peruvian economic policy has been based on a kind of blind optimism, shared frequently by the World Bank and international bankers,[6] that has persisted long after economic realities should have made it apparent that expectations were not going to be met.

During the 1970s, international liquidity allowed the size of the public sector to double, and, as a consequence, the overall performance of the economy declined. Successive governments chose the easy way of borrowing rather than imposing fiscal discipline to make up for shortfalls caused by stagnating agricultural productivity and the poorly coordinated expansion of the state. Ambitious investment projects, which seldom have had a good return, have been part of the unwise expansion as have arms buildups that always seem to be requested in the very worst of economic times as the unrest due to economic turmoil creates a demand for an increased sense of security.

As a result, Peruvian growth was about half the average of the major

Latin American countries. Through decades of weak development for the entire region, Peru's income per capita ranking in Latin America fell from seventh place in 1960 to fourteenth in 1985.

Economic policies through all these years have swung, sometimes like a pendulum, between opposite poles: the structuralist scheme embodied originally by ECLA (United Nations Economic Commission for Latin America) on the one hand, and the neoclassical or orthodox approach on the other. According to Schydlowsky and Juan Julio Wicht:

> The ECLA-structuralist model emphasizes that the underdeveloped economies (the periphery) suffer from a structural insufficiency of internal demand and external dependency which ought to be overcome by means of import substitution industrialization, fixed exchange rates, price controls, and growth of fiscal expenditures. At the opposite pole the monetarist model attempts to correct inflation and external and fiscal deficits (created by the former model) with a strong reduction of demand, devaluations, credit restrictions, elimination of subsidies, etc. This is certainly a very simplified presentation of these models, but there is a certain amount of truth in this synthesis: the structuralists want to increase domestic supply and insist on social and political aspects with frequent neglect of economic factors, thus opening wide gaps (e.g., savings-investment, or government deficit spending); the monetarists see the problem from the point of view of closing the deficits, and in fact they see no other solution than that of suppressing demand (with the inevitable neglect of the social and the political).
>
> For the monetarist, development comes from monetary stability. Stability, in turn, is brought about by controlling aggregate demand. The structuralists, on the other hand, maintain that monetary stability is a by-product of development. They claim that the monetarist cure would kill development. It would require a substantial rise in unemployment and a drop in consumption to bring down sticky prices. Structuralists would attack supply rigidities instead. Inflation, according to their game plan, is acceptable as the only alternative to stagnation—the result of any attempt to stabilize prices. Inflation can be used as an instrument to increase capital formation, one that usually substitutes state for private resources and management.[7]

During the 1970s and the early 1980s, foreign credit made it possible for Peru, caught up in a maze of frustrated social transformations, to consume and poorly invest far more than it actually produced. Exports failed to grow at a pace sufficient to provide the foreign exchange needed for imports and to comply with increasing foreign-debt-servicing commitments.

During the 1980s, Peru's only boom export product has been illicit:

coca. Worth now approximately US$1 billion a year, coca provides more foreign exchange to the country than any of its legal exports. As a result of inflation and negative interest rates, domestic savings have fallen and are insufficient to finance ongoing investment projects, several of which have lacked even a modicum of economic rationality. Hit by various limitations, including empiricism, centralism, and sheer unwieldiness, the state apparatus has failed to generate the resources needed to fulfill even its basic functions. The country is currently affected by overall social and economic disorder.

For all these reasons, few people should have been surprised that in the second half of 1984, as the international financial system ceased granting new loans to Peru, its government began defaulting on its commitments abroad. As of mid-1985, Peru was about US$1.8 billion behind in the service of its debt, and it was estimated that the total payments due at the end of the year would be approximately US$3.5 billion, or about 10 percent more than expected export revenue for the year. Moreover, a political change had taken place that would have enormous economic repercussions.

3 / The Political Situation in Peru Today

On July 28, 1985, thirty-six-year-old Alan Garcia Perez was sworn in as president of Peru, becoming the youngest chief executive in the world. In his inaugural address, President Garcia announced that in the future Peru would pay no more than 10 percent of its export earnings to meet debt-service obligations on some $14 billion of international debts.* The rest of the world was left to wonder who Alan Garcia was and how that 10 percent figure was arrived at.

Profile of a Populist Leader

Although his administration is no longer brand-new, most Peruvians still hesitate before attempting to answer the question, Who is Alan Garcia? As a politician, he is unpredictable, a complex mixture of rational statesman and emotional revolutionary. His popular charisma is as powerful as Peron's was in Argentina or Castro's has been in Cuba. He clearly sees himself as Peru's messiah: when he was a graduate student just back from Europe, he drove along Lima's expressway at 100 miles per hour, joking to his worried companions, "Nothing can happen to us. I first have to become President of Peru."

Politics have always been part of Garcia's life. He belongs, and at the same time doesn't belong, to the APRA party. He is a third-generation *aprista*—his parents and grandmother are *apristas*—which is a rare and useful credential in an organization so full of rituals and caught up, like Peru itself, in its past. Garcia was five years old when he first met his father, imprisoned throughout his son's infancy for being a minor *aprista* leader. As president, he took his father with him to an emotional ceremony in which he closed a prison in downtown Lima where many

* For a picture of the debt problem in Peru at the end of 1987, see Appendix 2.

other *apristas* had been held because of their political ideas. His family belongs to the Peruvian middle class (his mother is a high school teacher); none of its members had ever held a position of power before 1985. These origins are a point of pride with him, an unusual attitude in a country sometimes saturated by colonial aristocratic nostalgia.

Garcia was a late developer. Although some of his political interests were evident as a youth, when he became a member of Haya de la Torre's inner circle, his academic credentials are not at all impressive. He studied law in Lima and sociology in Madrid and Paris, where he led a sort of bohemian life until his late twenties, occasionally playing the guitar and singing Mexican music for meals at a small restaurant in Paris (he revisited the restaurant as president-elect for a private surprise party). While in Madrid he met his current wife—Pilar Nores, an Argentine economist from a well-known Cordoba family.

Rather than being the product of a given university, Garcia is a graduate of the intellectual environment of European cafes. It was there that he formed his political convictions and gained a reputation among young *apristas*. Through these years, he kept in close touch with the leadership of APRA.

Although Garcia is capable of pragmatic analysis, he is also a follower of the "dependency theory" that explains Latin America's lack of development in terms of exploitation of labor and resources. According to Howard Wiarda and Harvey Kline, however, there are many kinds of dependency theorists in Latin America:

> One group sees the separation of an industrialized North from a primary-product-oriented South as a result of a conspiracy. . . . Others see it more as a natural and inevitable happening. They argue that the development of the North and the underdevelopment of Latin America and the rest of the Third World go hand in hand.[1]

Being president is Garcia's first full-time job. In 1978, he was called by Haya de la Torre to participate in the elections for the constituent assembly. He was one of a hundred chosen to participate in this assembly, called for the purpose of creating a new constitution. Then in 1980, in an election campaign that taught him how to negotiate the corridors of internal party politics, he was elected as a deputy for Lima. His record as a congressman was rather disappointing, primarily because he neglected legislative duties in order to concentrate on a bold bid to fill the power vacuum in the party left by Haya de la Torre's death in 1979;

the vacuum had been created by infighting among the older generation of *apristas*. The defeat of APRA's presidential candidate in the 1980 election also opened the doors to a young charismatic leader who was not averse to risks in his quest for power.

Garcia is a workaholic, rushing through twenty-hour days filled with activities. There were days during the campaign when he appeared at five or six mass meetings, and spoke for more than an hour at each. Assistants got tired just trying to keep up. He also has a tendency to try to do everything himself. For example, although the Peruvian Constitution endows ministers with formal responsibility for all government acts—it does not hold the president responsible for them—Garcia treats most of his ministers as second-class secretaries, calling them in the middle of the night to request information for his own use.

Garcia, when he is interested in a subject, has shown a marked ability to learn fast. Until a few years ago, for instance, he was rather unfamiliar with U.S. politics and the nuances of governing, and knew little about the intricacies of international trade and capital markets. He has quickly remedied that and continues to make good use of his personal strengths to accumulate the knowledge needed for governing. In fact, his informal style of questioning as well as his extraordinary memory have often embarrassed occasional informants who have attempted to lecture him.

On a one-to-one basis, Garcia is a first-class conversationalist; however, the minute he has an audience, he tends to start playing politics, sending messages between the lines and playing one participant against another, sometimes just for the fun of it. If the media, particularly television, is present, he can instantly engage in an easy dialogue with his entire constituency. He is always anxious to be in the limelight, and his activities are given broad coverage on television every night. Peru's top humorist, Sofocleto, has nicknamed Garcia "Crazy Horse," a good description of his wild energy and abrasive personality.

Some of Garcia's domestic proposals make a great deal of sense, but he often contradicts himself. For example, although aware that the expansion of the state cannot be sustained, he nationalized the entire domestic banking system for the sake of gaining control of credit. Although he seems to have a broad vision of the future, his economic policies, up to now, have been strictly short-term.

Garcia is much more an emotional leader than a rational ideologue. The position of APRA was considered center-right when he was a student in his late teens. For his presidential campaign, he chose the slogan "nationalist, democratic, and popular" to characterize his future government. "Anti-imperialist" was another slogan in his original campaign plan, but it was dropped because the polls showed it did not evoke as much general consensus. In reading and forming public moods, Garcia acts as a professional politician.

There are two areas in which Garcia's concerns are clear: the need to govern for the poor, the marginal, the peasants; and the need to push these concerns at the international level. He does not consider himself a "manager of development but a transformer of society." Garcia has an urge to be a Third World leader, neither capitalist nor Communist but in some way related to the international socialists.

Everything Garcia says and does needs to be carefully examined; little is straightforward. For example, his government has had a good formal record regarding freedom of the press; however, Garcia himself uses all his seductive powers behind the scene with several key journalists in order to guide public opinion in the direction of his goals. Examples of confusing behavior on his part abound. Against prevailing opinion in his party, Garcia made a political alliance with the insignificant Peruvian Christian Democrat party whose main leader, a personal friend of Garcia from his university years, became his minister of justice for two years.

Garcia is viewed with mixed feelings by his Latin American peers. Some, to his right, consider him a populist demagogue. Others—like Presidents Alfonsin, Sarney, Paz Estenssoro, Sanguinetti—who might have been more sympathetic to his appeals and demands, have on occasion been upset by his abrasive personality. On formal state visits, he easily gets involved in controversial domestic issues. Wherever he goes, his long-run objective is to make an impression on the people, especially the young. Garcia is planning ahead, looking for a regional audience for the time when most current Latin American leaders have vanished from the political scene. A much better candidate than administrator, Garcia is running to become a kind of Latin American statesman of the twenty-first century.

His only major regional supporter, who thinks of Garcia as his own protege, is Carlos Andres Perez, the former and newly reelected president of Venezuela. Although Perez is worried by Garcia's weak grip on economic matters, he is confident of Garcia's future role in Latin America and is a full supporter of his political rhetoric. It was on Perez's advice that Garcia bypassed his party in selecting a professional diplomat as his minister of foreign affairs. However, Garcia's attempt to become the president of the nonaligned movement in 1989 failed because of the economic crisis Peru is facing. In any case, Fidel Castro, who has a strong influence on most African countries, was likely to veto someone with an ego as great as his own.

Garcia has gotten a mixed response from European statesmen like Bettino Craxi, Francois Mitterrand, and Felipe Gonzalez. The Spanish prime minister, for instance, who might have considered himself a political and spiritual ally of Garcia, felt somewhat uneasy when the Peruvian president, in one of his typical impromptus, almost kidnapped him in his car for a stopover visit to Lima's slums as well as for an unprogrammed private flight to Cuzco while their finance ministers were getting nowhere in an embarrassing discussion regarding Peru's debt arrears to Spain.

In terms of Garcia's relations with the United States, there is an uneasiness that dates back to his inauguration. James A. Baker III, as secretary of the Treasury, went to Peru to attend the inauguration. While there he took the opportunity to hold a series of discussions of the debt situation with some Latin American presidents, who were also in Peru for the inauguration; this was a few weeks before he was to launch his debt plan at the IMF meeting in Seoul. Robin Broad, then at the U.S. Treasury, wrote in *The New York Times* that the Baker Plan was simply "an attempt to steal the thunder from the new Peruvian president."

In a typical gesture aimed at saving time, Baker, who wanted to return to Washington as soon as possible, insisted on having breakfast with the president-elect on the day of his inauguration in order to avoid the ceremonial rituals that were to be held in the Peruvian Congress later in the day. For Garcia, as well as for many Peruvians, such a demand smacked of a lack of formality and respect for the solemn and democratic transition of powers. Garcia became even more upset when Baker's security personnel insisted that Garcia's house would have to be searched before the meeting. Garcia refused, and they did not meet until after Garcia's long inauguration speech in Congress. At that point, Baker was clearly bored and in a hurry, further angering Garcia.

Garcia had a chance to show his anger some months later when he came to New York to deliver a speech at the United Nations. He intended to raise issues that would provoke a U.S. reaction and he succeeded; after the speech, he had a harsh interchange of words with Secretary of State George Shultz about it. Garcia, who is interested in leaving an impression on his interlocutor, will sometimes overstep the bounds of propriety to do so. He prefers Shultz, or anyone for that matter, to clearly remember him, for better or worse, than to pass unnoticed amid one hundred and sixty heads of state.

The "10 Percent Default"

The second question raised by the 1985 inauguration speech was, What does 10 percent mean? Trying to answer that is as difficult as explaining who Garcia is. The answer lies in the development of the campaign and the character and plans of Garcia.

When explaining the term, Garcia's spokesmen point out that in 1933, Haya de la Torre said:

> Let us not forget that the APRA party has, for three years now, held that Peru could not solve its economic difficulties with foreign creditors without doing what Mexico did, summoning a banker's commission—not to receive lessons, but rather to demonstrate to them the payment inability of the country. . . . I am very familiar with the outcome of the negotiations with the international bankers commission in Mexico; our pseudostatesmen should learn a lot of the excellent achievements obtained by Mexican technocrats. Peru, like Mexico, needs to secure its payment ability with a legal norm inspired in the wise Mexican principle: Foreign debt service payments should never exceed 10 percent of the federal budget.[2]

Apristas have sometimes argued that this was the precedent for Garcia's establishment, half a century later, of the same limit for Peru's debt service.

The quote, however, was only rediscovered by *apristas* after Garcia's inauguration speech. Haya de la Torre was a wise man, but he often contradicted himself. For instance, on a later occasion—a speech on October 9, 1945, presenting APRA's economic program—he said:

> We cannot avoid being part of the continental and worldwide economic context. At the same time, we are compelled to solve internal problems that in many ways will be more difficult to solve if we proclaim ourselves the Robinson Crusoe of a new island that does not import, export nor pay.[3]

Because Haya de la Torre's thoughts on repayment of debt were subject to differing interpretations, he is unlikely to have been the inspiration for Garcia's inaugural initiative.

A logical place to search for the origins of Garcia's "10 percent rule" is the APRA platform for governing, and the thoughts of the men who helped shape it. In his bid for APRA's presidential candidacy,

Garcia required the support of his generation. This was granted by the endorsement of Luis Alva Castro, a true party man in his early forties. Though of the same generation as Garcia, Alva went to prison for opposing the military government while Garcia was in Europe enjoying student life.

Garcia seduced the *apristas* as a group by his imagination, his conviction, and his ability to lead them to victory after sixty years of political struggle. Alva, not a charismatic personality, instead makes deals behind the scene, one by one, with each leader of the party. They are both, however, professional politicians and aware of their respective strengths and limitations.

Alva was—at least in theory—in charge of Garcia's campaign. He also presided over the CONAPLAN, a committee in charge of drafting a government plan. In accordance with Alva's style, CONAPLAN was more an excuse for the gathering together of technocrats as well as of different representatives of special interests than a working institution in search of coherent policies. Garcia needed no platform for the campaign; his charm and slogans were more than enough for winning the election.

The CONAPLAN did come up with more than a thousand pages of drafts, including different proposals for almost every policy area. Editing them into a common framework was an almost impossible job for which Alva lacked both enough talent and enthusiasm. It would have forced APRA to choose, before the election, between different alternatives at a time when they were promising a "government for all Peruvians."

In terms of foreign debt, however, most drafts of CONAPLAN read the same:

> *Foreign Debt*
>
> *Main Objective:* To reschedule in the long run the service of the foreign debt and to obtain the new credits the country needs in conditions that are favorable to its development.
>
> *Policy Guidelines:*
>
> a) Payment of the foreign debt service is impossible under current conditions. A renegotiation should be called for immediately to avoid paying more than 20% of exports.
>
> b) Efforts should be made to agree on a better debt negotiation position with other Latin American debtors.
>
> c) Financial costs should be reduced significantly.

d) Debt relief measures should be complemented by actions in favor of better international prices for raw materials, an increase in international liquidity and lower protectionism in industrialized countries.

e) Debt payments in kind should be promoted.

f) New debt should be more diversified in terms of both countries and sources.

g) Long term debt with international agencies should be preferred to other sources.

h) New indebtedness should be concentrated in projects which generate or save foreign exchange.[4]

Garcia had, in addition to Alva's CONAPLAN, a set of advisers who held somewhat different points of view on what needed to be done about Peru's economy. On the one hand, there were the views of Manuel Moreyra, a successful former chairman of the Central Bank, who supported a complex, orthodox-in/heterodox-out kind of economic policy that called for a coherent stabilization program accompanied by an international denunciation of the incompetence of the IMF in dealing with the Peruvian situation. The other approach, supported mainly by Carlos Franco, an ideologist of the Velasco left-wing military government, and by Daniel Carbonetto, an Argentine technocrat linked to the Peronist party, called for a new, revised, and improved (but enacted at a slower pace) set of the kind of populist measures that Salvador Allende enacted in Chile. Once again in Peruvian politics, a conflict developed between pragmatists and idealists, between what was feasible and what was desirable. The latter won, as was expected.

Garcia did not visit the CONAPLAN offices until he was president-elect. From the group he picked out a few names for his cabinet and some ideas. During the last months of President Belaunde's term, President Alfonsin paid a courtesy visit to Peru in return for Belaunde's support for Argentina during the Malvinas-Falklands war. At a private meeting, Garcia suggested to Alfonsin that the two countries should form a common front on the debt issue. But the Austral Plan—the first heterodox attempt in Argentina to stop inflation with fiscal discipline and controls—was already in the making, and secret conversations were being held in Washington with a view to gaining IMF support for it. Alfonsin, therefore, declined to join in a debt cartel. Some weeks later, and just days before his inauguration, Garcia noted with surprise the popular support Alfonsin obtained by applying the Austral Plan and began to seek more information about it.

At the same time, Garcia was busy playing "musical chairs" in naming his first cabinet. The very day of their election—Garcia as president, Alva as deputy and second vice president (Peru elects two vice presidents)—Garcia's and Alva's long-run personal goals diverged. Garcia began to contemplate seeking passage of a constitutional amendment that would enable his reelection in 1990 (currently a president may not serve consecutive terms). Alva saw himself as the front-runner for that nomination.

As part of this love-hate relationship, Garcia forced Alva, against his will, to accept the position of minister of economy and finance (and premier) in his first cabinet. It is generally believed in Latin America that such a job is a trap for anyone with further political aspirations; Latin America's economic ministers are either unpopular or incompetent. Alva—with the advice of Richard Webb, chairman of the Peruvian central bank during the previous administration; his CONAPLAN team; and a group of Garcia's radical supporters—was put in the position of having to assemble an emergency economic program during a three-day summit at an elegant Lima hotel. He managed to reach a compromise on domestic policies between the more "cautious" group —himself, his appointed vice-minister Leonel Figueroa, Webb—and the "audacious" group supported by the president, but little was decided regarding the debt service.

Garcia's inaugural speech on July 28, 1985, called for a debt-service limit of 10 percent of exports during the first year of his government and was especially critical of the IMF procedures, demanding a change in its institutional policies. It is hard to believe that Garcia was, at that time, rereading Haya de la Torre—or anyone else. He was playing high-risk politics. He had asked how much had been paid during Belaunde's last year in government, and when the answer turned out to be 13 percent, he considered it reasonable to openly demand better treatment from the international community than was given his predecessor.

Some analysts believed that Peru had little to lose by this attitude, since its creditors were unlikely to wish to lend more money to the country anyway. Net resource transfer had been negative since 1984 and was unlikely to become positive for the foreseeable future—even if Peru were to behave like an impeccable debtor. The imposition of the 10 percent ceiling, however, provoked a mixture of sympathy and apprehension in world financial markets; they recognized that Peru faced particularly difficult circumstances, while at the same time they were concerned that other debtors might adopt a similar unilateral stance.

But Garcia's policy has hardly been imitated by other debtors. It took only a short time for the international community to discover that there was little of substance behind the Peruvian rhetoric. The country's economic planners simply had not done any homework to come up with new ideas for refinancing the national debt. In the absence of detailed alternative proposals, it was easy for the global financial system to convince other debtors that Peru could have acquired a great deal more by playing by the rules.

On November 1985, Peru's debt was declared "value-impaired" by the U.S. authorities, who had avoided taking this step against the Belaunde government under the same circumstances because of what the American officials thought of as good-faith efforts. They had also naively expected that the incoming Garcia government would follow a more orthodox view regarding the debt than had his predecessor. When Garcia maintained the same level of payment—and even questioned his creditors' right to request payment—the declaration was finally seen as necessary.

Alva was somewhat unprepared for handling Garcia's debt initiative. A conflict developed between Alva's more "cautious" team and the "audacious" presidential advisers. Both sides, however, lacked financial experience. When Alva went to the IMF annual meeting in Seoul in October 1985, there was a general expectation in the international financial community that he would put forth a coherent proposal regarding Peru's debt, one of the basic topics addressed by Garcia in his previous presentation to the United Nations. Instead, Alva's speech to the IMF, aimed primarily at domestic consumption, turned out to be a repetition of political cliches with little technical justification of the criteria followed by the Peruvian government.

In spite of Alva's vagueness, by this time some qualifications had been added to the "10 percent theory": first, all payments in kind, payments to Latin American governments and agencies, and all short-term debt were to be excluded from the 10 percent limit; second, priority was to be given to lenders who provided net financial inflows. The ceiling, after all, was a global one that did not necessarily apply to any single creditor or group of creditors. Priorities, however, were never clearly stated, and payments have in practice been decided on a day-to-day basis.

Thus, for the first two years of Garcia's government, Peru remained—with the exception of relatively short-lived lapses—current in its payments to the World Bank and the Inter-American Development Bank because the country was expecting disbursements of credits previously approved by these institutions. Peru also had been punctilious in servicing in kind most of its debt to the Soviet Union. Furthermore, the government has met its USAID repayment schedules in timely fashion to avoid enforcement of regulations such as the Brooke-Alexander Amendment, which would cut off even loans for food in the case of a moratorium. Despite the government rhetoric, and the running sore of disputes concerning compensation for the nationalization of Belco Petroleum Co., U.S. bilateral aid to Peru has been continued, although at much lower levels. At a congressional hearing, Elliott Abrams, assistant secretary of state, declared:

> For over a year, Peru has carried on a serious and successful campaign against narcotics traffickers. But this campaign draws on scarce resources. Both our military and economic assistance requests are essential if we are to achieve cooperation on the antinarcotics front and improve our dialogue with Peru on the management of its economic and debt crises. By improving our overall relationship with Peru, this assistance will act to counter Soviet influence, particularly with the military.

Besides the commercial banks, the most publicized victim of the 10 percent ceiling has been, of course, the International Monetary Fund. By allowing arrears to the Fund to accumulate, Peru has challenged one of the fundamental rules of international finance.

By August 1986, arrears to the IMF had reached more than $200 million. In April 1986, the Fund threatened to declare Peru ineligible for further credit—a condition that could have had a significant effect on the World Bank, Inter-American Development Bank, and several commercial creditors' transactions. In response, the Peruvians offered a partial payment of $35 million. Under pressure from the Reagan administration, and against the powerfully expressed advice of his own staff, the managing director of the Fund, Jacques de Larosiere, said he would advise the board of directors to accept the partial payment, on the strict understanding that Peru should undertake solemnly on May 6 to pay all its arrears by August 15; otherwise, the country would be declared ineligible automatically. Peru's representative at the Fund, Jaysuno Abramovich, did indeed make such a promise.

Two days prior to the August 15 deadline, the Peruvian government made a payment to the Fund of $35 million, accompanied by a cable saying that this was a significant addition to the payment made in April, that it would be imprudent in the present circumstances "to attempt to repay in full, and that Peru hoped the Fund would understand."

By then, Garcia had publicly reaffirmed the 10 percent ceiling in his first State of the Nation speech (July 28, 1986), giving it further support by announcing the suspension of all service payments for two years on the private sector's $1.5 billion foreign debt, and of all profit remittances by foreign-owned corporations operating in Peru. This time, the Fund's patience was finally exhausted. At a board meeting held on the morning of August 15, Peru was declared ineligible. The discussion, such as it was, apparently lasted only a few minutes.

10 Percent and the Real World

Any casual observer of the world debt situation, if asked how much of its public foreign debt has Peru been paying since 1985, would probably answer zero. This popular perception is false. As a matter of fact, the 10 percent ceiling had to be defined to include services among exports and to exclude some kinds of payment in order to make actual payments fit under the 10 percent limit. During 1986, for instance, according to official sources, total payments were over $600 million; 17 percent of total exports (see Table 3.1). Payments counted under the 10 percent limit came to 11.7 percent of exports, so the span of time was redefined in order to reduce this coefficient to 9.2 percent of exports in the period August 1985-July 1986 (the first year of Garcia's administration) and 9.7 percent in the following year.

An effort was made then to honor the service of the debt, and, Garcia's rhetoric to the contrary, payments did not change much. In comparison to payments in 1984, the problem was made worse, however, by the absence of coherent and consistent criteria for the handling of the overall strategy for debt negotiation. Namely, expecting a net inflow of capital (based on the erroneous assumption that Peru could selectively default against certain lending institutions while staying on good terms with others), the government found, by the end of 1986, that net flows of capital related to the foreign debt had been negative by $151.2 million during that year (see Table 3.2).

What had gone wrong? Very simple: multilateral institutions delayed pending disbursements, and a lack of new financing reversed the flow of the transfers from these organizations. Likewise, as a result of payments in kind, a turnaround took place in the net transfer of resources from socialist countries. Only some governments and agencies, the U.S. government included among them, as well as other creditors whose loans were guaranteed by their respective governments generated some capital inflows (see Table 3.3).

Table 3.1
Public Foreign Debt Service (US$ Million)

	Total Aug.–Dec. 1985	*Total 1986*	*Total Aug. 1985– July 1986*	*Total 1987*	*Total Aug. 1986– July 1987*
A. Payments included in 10 percent limit:	*132.5*	*385.2*	*322.0*	*258.3*	*323.9*
Multilateral Organizations	104.7	302.9	243.0	145.8	260.1
1. Inter-American Development Bank	35.9	86.1	58.6	97.4	111.6
2. World Bank	39.5	141.6	115.5	46.8	112.4
3. IFAD[a]	0.2	1.2	0.8	1.6	0.6
4. IMF	29.1	74.0	68.1	0.0	33.0
Food	5.6	8.5	14.0	0.1	0.2
Governments	13.3	38.3	32.5	67.0	50.3
1. Europe	7.8	1.0	8.1	18.8	2.0
2. U.S.[b]	1.4	37.2	20.3	41.0	41.0
3. Others	4.1	0.1	4.1	7.2	7.3
Commercial Banks	8.0	27.5	28.3	4.7	7.6
Others	0.9	8.0	4.2	40.7	5.9
Exports of Goods and Services	1628.0	3305.0	3512.0	3518.0	3346.0
Debt Service/Exports (%)	8.1	11.7	9.2	7.3	9.7
B. Payments not included:	*116.9*	*271.3*	*275.2*	*220.8*	*220.5*
Multilateral Organizations	43.0	78.2	84.6	41.5	73.4
1. Corporacion Andina de Fomento	5.0	7.1	10.0	8.0	5.4
2. Fondo Andino de Reservas	38.0	71.1	74.6	33.5	68.0
LAFTA[c] agreements	16.9	66.9	56.1	62.0	50.0
Payments in kind	48.2	107.6	116.2	96.5	75.2
Other payments	8.8	18.6	18.3	20.7	21.8
Total Public Debt Service (A + B)/Exports	15.3	17.0	—	16.3	—

Source: The author, from semiofficial information.

a. International Fund for Agricultural Development

b. Including PL480

c. Latin American Free Trade Association

Table 3.2
Public Foreign Debt (US$ Million)

	Aug.-Dec. 1985	*1986*	*Jan.-Jun. 1987*	*Total*
Total Payments[a]	240.6	635.9	234.3	1110.8
New Disbursements	314.8	484.7	170.3	969.8
Difference	74.2	(151.2)	(64.0)	(141.0)

Source: A confidential official document.
a. These totals differ marginally from those on Table 3.1 because of minor differences in nomenclature and sources.

Table 3.3
Net Real Flow by Type of Creditor[a] (US$ Million)

	1983	*1984*	*1985*	*1986*
I. Long Term				
1. Public Sector	803	560	43	- 93
a) Government and Governmental Agencies (Paris Club)	24	98	175	51
b) Commercial Banks	145	201	- 128	- 21
c) Multilateral Organizations	109	125	27	- 69
d) The Soviet Union and East Bloc	87	- 58	- 123	- 79
e) Private Suppliers	438	194	92	25
2. Private Sector	- 265	- 285	- 247	- 98
3. Central Reserve Bank	338	- 280	- 179	- 146[b]
II. Short Term Public and Private	- 771	- 365	- 335	+ 77
Total Net Flow	105	- 370	- 718	- 260

a. Disbursements minus amortizations and interest that have effectively been paid. These figures differ a bit from previous tables because they include debt of the private sector. Also there are minor differences because of different sources and nomenclature.
b. If short-term debt of the Central Bank included in II is considered, the subtotal becomes much lower.
Source: Drago Kisic, *De la Corresponsabilidad a la Moratoria: El Caso de la Deuda Externa Peruana 1970-1986,* July 1987. Edited by Centro Peruano de Estudios Internacionales (CEPEI).

Adding to the problem was the situation regarding commercial banks. Since commercial banks did not offer new disbursements, they have only received "good will" payments. In September 1986, a meeting was held between the advisory committee of the 260 creditor banks and representatives of the Peruvian government. On that occasion, the government was planning to present a proposal for rescheduling with a twenty- to thirty-year repayment period with five to ten years of grace, including a significant reduction in interest rates. On the private recommendation of advisers, the government postponed such demands since they only would have further hurt relations with the bank's steering committee.

Early in 1987, further conflict between the followers of Garcia and Alva added to Peru's problems. The president's "audacious" group ousted the pro-Alva authorities of the central bank, who wanted to cool down an increasingly overheated economy. Some months later, Alva resigned, but he was soon elected, against Garcia's wishes, president of the Chamber of Deputies.

Then, complicating and worsening the problems, Garcia, in his second State of the Nation speech delivered on July 28, 1987, in addition to proposing the nationalization of all domestic banking, restated his intention of limiting debt payments in accordance with export revenues; the only saving grace was that, for the first time, he did not insist on a given figure and accepted the possibility of debt-for-equity swaps (the regulations for these were not approved until October 1988), or other similar deals, for new investment projects related to exports.

4 / The Current Economic Situation in Peru

An outstanding Peruvian historian born at the turn of the century, Jorge Basadre, called Peru a land of lost opportunities. He finished a monumental, twenty-volume work on Peru with the question: "What is, after all, Peru?" And went on to answer: "A beautiful promise yet to be fulfilled."

Some decades later, this idea of future promise was replaced by a feeling of having fallen under a divine curse. "When did Peru get all screwed up?" is the most cited quote of a fictional character in one of Mario Vargas Llosa's novels describing the Peru of the fifties. But in the 1950s, Peru's economic position in Latin America was good. It was only over the last quarter of a century that the country experienced—to a greater extent that most other Latin American countries—a significant decline. (For detailed comparisons of Peru and her Latin American neighbors, see Appendix 3.) The per capita income in real terms has now returned to what it was at the beginning of the sixties after a period of demographic explosion, significant migration to the capital city, inefficient agrarian reform, and an enormous expansion of the state.

Moreover, growth of gross domestic product (GDP) per capita (in current US$), consumption per capita, and public and private investment fell progressively over the three five-year periods since 1970 (see Table 4.1).

This extremely poor performance stands in sharp contrast to average real GDP growth of 5.5 percent a year between 1950 and 1970—with bursts of 6.0 and 7.2 percent growth in 1950-55 and 1960-65.

Figures like these led many of Garcia's advisers to conclude, erroneously in my view, that Peru has followed poor policies since 1976—notably in liberalizing foreign trade after 1978—and to recommend that Peru revert to the inward-looking policies of 1971-75, which produced growth greater than that in any subsequent period. However, the policies followed at that time— acceptance of an increasingly overvalued exchange rate, declining exports, and rapidly rising imports brought, as has been shown, a major balance of payments crisis.

It is also important to remember that growth during 1971-75 was fostered by excessive increases in externally financed public investment and by an initial boost to investment and industrial output from import substitution. Neither policy was indefinitely sustainable nor was either the basis for sound long-term growth. Furthermore, growth slowed in this period compared with the two preceding decades. Indeed, much of Peru's poor economic performance over the past decade is, in my opinion, a consequence of the structural changes made in the 1968-75 period by the first phase of the military government; these were only made worse by misapplied government borrowing, poor-quality public investment, excessive defense expenditures, and erratic and inconsistent macroeconomic policies.

From that period on, gross (current and capital) public expenditures rose from 22 percent of GDP (1970) to 51 percent (1985). Public-sector employment (including armed forces) increased at almost three times the rate of overall employment growth. This process, together with other centripetal forces (including high industrial tariffs), exacerbated the problems facing the government. An additional problem was the growing concentration of population in and around Lima as a result of growing public-sector employment (Lima's share of that employment increased from 38 percent in the 1960s to over 45 percent today). The problem

Table 4.1
Growth Rate of Key Variables

	1971–75	*1976–80*	*1981–85*
GDP	5.3	1.7	- 0.2
GDP per capita (in current US$)	12.3	4.4	- 4.8
Public Consumption per capita	5.4	- 1.6	- 4.0
Private Consumption per capita	2.2	- 0.6	- 3.6
Public Sector Gross Fixed Investment	23.4	- 6.4	- 7.1
Private Sector Gross Fixed Investment	10.5	- 6.3	- 8.9
Exports	5.9	24.1	- 3.7
Imports	28.3	6.6	- 5.7

Source: Derived from Appendix 1.

has been further complicated by the avalanche of peasants coming down from the sierra. (An unrealistic exchange rate and direct subsidies for food importers undermined the profitability of domestic agriculture.) The government has not coped well with the expanding urban population, giving rise to an enormous expansion of the underground economy. One result of increased public-sector employment is that real gross fixed capital formation rose almost three times as fast in the public sector as it did in the private sector during the last fifteen years, causing Peru's incremental capital/output ratio to rise precipitously.

In addition, the number of state-owned enterprises mushroomed over the past two decades: in 1968, there were less than 30 (partly or fully owned); by 1985, the number had risen to more than 200. Most of these enterprises have been taken over from private owners. State-owned enterprises, which are to be found in most sectors of the economy, are estimated to account currently for about 20 percent of GDP, but their overall economic influence is much greater since they also dominate large areas of private decisionmaking. Many are inefficient and face little or no competition. Most are politically controlled and are not required to economize their use of resources, make a profit, undertake investments that pay for themselves, or service their debts.

The state has, therefore, become the great national patron, replacing the local landowners and oligarchs of the past. It is from the state and its head that jobs, patronage, money, and favors flow, and political disputes tend to be handled administratively and bureaucratically, rather than through the open competition of party politics.

A Critical Turning Point

The year 1986 marked a critical juncture for Peru economically. The nation had to face the problems created by a history of steady borrowing abroad. In addition to limiting debt service, the government put in place an emergency economic program based on higher wages, lower taxes, public employment programs, and price and exchange controls. These measures allowed a significant expansion of internal demand and growth of the gross domestic product (see Table 4.2). It also brought, in the beginning, a reduction in inflation. Great efforts were made to improve the income of rural peasants, especially by paying higher prices for most agricultural products, which were later sold at a loss by the state. As a result of a rise in disposable income—up to 20 percent in real terms for many in the lower income levels—GDP grew by 8.5 percent in 1986, the highest rate for any Latin American country. However, as 1986 drew to a close, projections for both the external and fiscal sectors were worrisome.

Existing idle capacity and reduced interest rates and taxes, in addition to price controls and a freeze in the exchange rate for imports, forced down inflation from 158.3 percent in 1985 to 62.9 percent in 1986. However, it rebounded to 114.5 percent in 1987. The exchange freeze also led many to convert dollar-denominated certificates of deposit into local currency, although interest rates remained negative in real terms in the domestic banking system. In spite of an internal boom in production, total liquidity did not increase in real terms because of an increase in the velocity of money. The local stock market followed much the same pattern, flourishing for a brief time.

Although there was a covert devaluation of about 30 percent for non-traditional exports (against internal inflation of 62.9 percent) during 1986, total exports fell and imports, as could be expected, rocketed with the increase in aggregate demand, which should have been expected in a country whose domestic production of wheat, beef, and milk is rather insignificant (see Table 4.3).

A surplus of US$1 billion in the external balance of real resources (goods and services) in 1985 turned into a deficit of US$320 million in 1986 and a greater one of US$858 million in 1987. The deficit in the financial account was reduced, but with imports exceeding exports for

Table 4.2
Growth of Peruvian GDP

	Share of GDP (%)	*1985*	*1986*	*1987*
			Percentages	
Sectors				
Agricultural	14	2.3	3.7	7.9
Fishing	1	7.5	3.0	- 10.1
Mining	10	6.1	- 2.5	0.2
Manufacturing	22	4.1	17.8	11.0
Construction	4	- 13.1	21.2	13.7
Government	8	- 0.5	2.2	- 2.3
Others (commerce and others)	41	1.9	8.2	7.2
Total	100	1.9	8.5	6.9

Source: Central Bank figures.

the first time in years, services (the "invisibles" in the current account, including the partial service of the external debt) had to be paid for out of accumulated reserves. As a result, these went down by US$459 million in 1986 and by US$806 million in 1987.

Of course, as has always happened in similar situations, there were people paying the bill: international creditors, who reacted by closing their doors to Peru; exporters, who according to government theorists would export the same amount no matter what the exchange rate was; savers, who were unwittingly subsidizing consumers; and the state itself, whose deficit (beyond the transitional savings in the service of the foreign debt), fueled by expansionary tax policies, was so great it resorted again to printing money.

The public-sector deficit almost doubled in 1986 and increased again in 1987, not because of an increase in current expenditures or capital investment, but because of a reduction of taxes and a freeze in prices and tariffs on services and goods provided by the state-owned enterprises (see Table 4.4). The need to finance internally 3 percent of GDP to cover

Table 4.3
Balance of Payments (US$ Million)

	1985	*1986*	*1987*
I. Balance of Real Resources	1,002	- 320	- 858
A. Trade Balance	1,172	- 16	- 463
1. Exports, f.o.b.	2,978	2,509	2,605
2. Imports, f.o.b.	1,806	2,525	3,068
B. Balance of Nontraditional Services	- 170	- 304	- 395
II. Financial Transfers	- 722	- 139	52
A. Unilateral Transfers	134	96	132
B. Financial Services and Long-Term Capital Flow	- 320	- 228	24
1. Public Sector	107	- 19	123
2. Private Sector	- 427	- 209	- 99
C. Short-Term Capital, Errors and Omissions	- 536	- 7	- 104
III. Change in Net International Reserves	280	- 459	- 806

Source: Reconstructed by the author, based on Central Reserve Bank figures.

the fiscal deficit in 1986 should have been a clear signal to call the consumer party to an end. By 1987, the situation was already out of control.

The government program should have been adjusted, during the first months of 1987, to avoid further gaps in production/demand, exports/imports, taxes/public expenditures, and savings/investment. However, against orthodox thinking, a self-proclaimed "audacious" economic team kept pushing wages up and interest rates down in an attempt to maintain previous growth rates.

As full capacity in the manufacturing sector was reached, the logical result was inflation: an average of 4 percent a month in 1986; 6 percent a month in the first six months of 1987; 8 percent a month in the second half of 1987. There was also a distortion of prices that induced everybody to borrow in domestic currency at low cost, using the money borrowed to buy cheap dollars, either greenbacks or imports of any kind. By July 1987, the exchange rate had jumped 50 percent in the parallel market.

To deal with this crisis, the government could have chosen either a "national agreement," which would have allowed a sharing of the cost of an adjustment program among all sectors, or a "populist radicalization" approach, which was aimed at complementing the economic turnaround with politically revolutionary measures. In his second State of

Table 4.4
Public-Sector Accounts (as percentage of GDP)

	1985	*1986*	*1987*
Central Government	- 4.0	- 6.2	- 9.6
Income	17.9	15.3	11.3
Expenditures[a]	21.9	21.5	21.0
Rest of the Public Sector	- 0.4	- 1.7	- 1.3
State-Owned Enterprises	- 0.6	- 2.0	- 1.7
Rest	0.2	0.3	0.4
Deficit of the Public Sector	- 4.4	- 7.9	- 10.9
External Financing	6.4	4.9	4.0
Internal Financing	- 2.0	3.0	6.9
Memorandum:			
Public Investment	7.3	6.1	5.0

Source: Estimated by the author, on the basis of official figures.
a. Includes the financial cost of arrears.

the Nation address—July 28, 1987—President Garcia enacted more controls, prohibited the free (parallel) market for foreign currency and, to the surprise of many, proposed the nationalization of all domestic banking. In doing so, Garcia was aware he was playing with fire. He had publicly rejected imposition of such measures while he was a candidate and in his 1986 State of the Nation speech. Moreover, during the months before this change in philosophy, he had been courting local bankers and entrepreneurs to persuade them to reinvest all their profits in Peru. Nationalization of the banks would be a slap in the face to them, but Garcia believed public opinion would again support him by an 80 percent majority, as it did after his initial confrontation with international bankers.

The reaction to his announcement did not meet Garcia's expectations. Local bankers fought back with the support of television and the press. Mario Vargas Llosa abandoned his writing to lead huge crowds in Peru's main cities against the proposal. The public originally split evenly on the issue, but when the law was finally passed, they were two to one against it. As a result, no bank has yet been formally nationalized. From the moment of Garcia's declaration of intent, many Peruvians started to believe that his autocratic style of government could be a threat in a country with fragile institutions and unstable democratic values.

With the nationalization of the banks, the government lost much of the credibility it had possessed only months before. On top of his confrontational rhetoric (which has been more upsetting to the international banking community than the partial default itself), the yet-to-be-paid-for expropriation of Belco Petroleum, and the menacing threat posed by the Sendero Luminoso (Shining Path) guerrillas and drug traffickers, the government of Garcia added to its troubles the increasing hostility of the local business community at a time when the correction of economic distortions of unprecedented magnitudes was needed. As *The Economist* said, "Alan Garcia is not Salvador Allende—yet."[1] And now his government is fighting a dramatic economic battle with little support. Cash reserves are nearly exhausted and inflation exceeded 100 percent a month in September 1988, the second-highest ever in the history of Latin America. Peru is approaching 1989 on the verge of total collapse.

The Price of Economic Turmoil

The past few years have been a period of increasing desperation and diminishing confidence in the future for most Peruvians. Although in my opinion the crisis the nation is facing has been caused mostly by internal mistakes, many Peruvians, still wedded to the "dependency" theory, put more blame on international developments beyond their control, which explains why the Marxist left ran second in 1985, and why its candidate, Alfonso Barrantes, is considered the front-runner for the presidency in 1990. It also helps explain the growth of Sendero Luminoso, considered by many the most radical and violent subversive group in the world today, and the belief held, according to a recent poll, by one out of every seven Peruvians that Sendero Luminoso could succeed some day. Few had held this belief earlier.

Throughout its history, the Peruvian state has not merely reflected the social structure, but has helped shape the class system through its control of economic and political resources. The state remains the principal regulator, coordinator, and pacesetter of the entire national system. That is why in Peru, as in most of Latin America, the competition for control of the state is so intense and sometimes violent. Determining who controls the pinnacles of the system is a fundamental, all-important, and virtually everyday preoccupation. Now, amid economic decline and widespread violence, Peru's middle class is becoming more pessimistic about the country's future and finds itself trying to assure its personal security in any way possible. Furthermore, with drug trade flourishing, corruption seems to have increased at all levels of society, weakening institutions as well as democratic values. More and more, young professionals are seeking to establish themselves abroad, most often in Canada and Spain. This brain drain may be the single most troublesome development for Peru's immediate future.

Nothing will stop the decline but a significant and sustained improvement in Peru's economic performance, and that seems unlikely unless the government agrees to confront and attack some of the critical problems facing it: the inefficiency of the state and its enterprises, the poor returns to public investment, the red tape that prevents competitiveness in the formal private sector, the widespread misallocation of labor and capital, the inadequate level of domestic savings, the low productivity of the underground economy, and so forth. And addressing these problems will take a minimum political consensus, which the crisis makes more and more difficult to achieve. A great effort will be necessary if Peru is to fulfill that "beautiful promise" Basadre spoke of.

5 / Conclusions

Given the vulnerability of the international financial system to Third World debt and the problems that that debt is causing for Third World nations, it is in the interest of everyone concerned to bring about an efficient adjustment. What is needed are reforms of domestic policies on the part of the debtor nations and adequate external financing to win time for these structural reforms to take hold.

Some time ago, Martin Feldstein calculated that if Brazil could achieve a 3.5 percent annual increase in its GDP and an equally high rate of increase in the growth of its exports while borrowing US$4 billion a year and paying 2.5 percent of GDP in debt service, its debt-to-export ratio would be reduced by half in ten years.[1] In discussing the Latin American region as a whole, I don't believe in such a rosy projection. For instance, since U.S. monetary and fiscal policies have not been brought into balance, there is a clear risk that the next move in interest rates will be up and not down. At the same time, exports from the debtor countries can only grow if the industrial world buys; unfortunately, there are fewer prospects for growth worldwide, and in countries like the United States, the principal world buyer, public sentiment for protectionism is gaining strength.

The problems facing the nations of Latin America, as Andres Bianchi and others have noted, have been compounded by their initial handling of their debt problems.[2] Even when their growing debts became impossible to ignore, most nations continued to put off domestic adjustment and continued to spend on public projects. The result was short-term growth at the cost of growing and unsustainable external disequilibria—and then, as in Peru now, a need for overadjustment, which might somewhat improve external accounts at the cost of a severe recession. An adequate adjustment should include not only expenditure reduction and a fall in imports but a reallocation of real resources from nontradables to exports or import substitution, either of which is necessarily a slower process.

In most countries in the region, debt indicators—such as the ratio of total debt to GDP, and of debt service to exports—have deteriorated markedly over the past few years as a consequence of these poorly designed adjustments, which give little scope for an efficient reallocation of resources. The net effect will be that the regional GDP per capita will be the same in 1990 as it was in 1980.

Yet in this process, debtors, creditors, and other interested parties have managed to find short-term solutions to seemingly insurmountable financial problems, and they appear willing to try out more new approaches for cushioning future crises. For example, the "menu of options" formula, including debt-into-equity swaps and exit bonds, has already become standard. Some other promising new ideas include the IMF's enhanced borrowing facility to help countries absorb external shocks like higher interest rates; buybacks of debt in the case of countries with severe problems, such as Peru; securitization of the principal of new loans; a loosening of the IMF's austerity strictures; and regulatory changes in the United States and other countries to permit, for example, capitalization of interest and other investment options for banks.

However, because of the length and severity of the crisis, now mixed up with the dramatic fall of stock prices on the world's exchanges, adjustment weariness has set in among debtors and debt fatigue among creditors. The former will be unable to postpone the demand for growth any longer; the latter will supply little, if any, new money. In the face of such an impasse, even the most promising ideas are, in the end, unlikely to prevent periodic moratoria, as in Peru.

It is up to the new U.S. administration to address this situation, recognizing that Latin American debt is more a political than an economic problem. A suspension/repudiation in other countries will, as in the case of Peru, be followed by recrimination, bad feelings, and disruption of trade. At that point, there will be time for little more than laying blame, and there will be more than enough blame to go around.

Unless new rules for the game are instituted, countries such as Peru, no matter what internal policies are applied, will remain outlaws for the next ten to twenty years when it comes to medium-term commercial credit. But regarding official and multilateral credit, a political arrangement of some kind must be made to enable debtors with deep economic problems and fragile democratic values and institutions to avoid yielding control to authoritarian or totalitarian regimes. The *outlaw complex*—"the Western World is against us"—that many Peruvians are increasingly feeling must be replaced by a *sense of belonging* to the community of Western nations, and the best way to do that is to provide debt relief in these special cases. If not, the temptation to rely increasingly on the Soviet bloc for further trade or business could increase with time.

Unfortunately, significant progress on the debt front, beyond the negotiations taking place with the World Bank in November 1988, seems improbable for Peru in the immediate future. Although Garcia's criterion of relating debt service to exports has been defended even by some orthodox analysts, like former IMF officer Walter Robichek, the common position in the international financial community may wrongly be to force Peru to pay the cost of breaking the rules.

The Negative Influence of International Debt

Since Peru's independence, the country has managed to survive despite repeatedly having no external credit for extended periods after declaring moratoriums on its foreign debt. And during each of these periods, growth has not been notably weaker than it was during periods in which international credit was available. The reason is that the main borrower has always been the Peruvian state, which has shown little ability to use such foreign credit to its benefit, instead designing policies that have accomplished little but turn the economy into a debt-addicted one.

Looking only at the latest crisis, where have all those billions borrowed gone in the last fifteen years? As seen earlier, the availability of foreign credit during the 1970s provided a cheap means of significantly increasing the Peruvian public sector's share of the economy; indeed, that sector grew much more, in relative terms, in Peru in that period than it did in the rest of Latin America. Currently, public debt accounts for about 90 percent of Peruvian foreign debt.

My own estimate is that the money went, in almost equal parts, to consumption and social services, defense expenditures, infrastructure, and productive projects. The first category, however, has not improved the living standards of the average Peruvian; social indicators have remained about the same for the past fifteen years. Regarding defense expenditures, as a percentage of GDP or of the total government budget, Peru has spent more than most other Latin American countries.[3] Also, the infrastructure projects undertaken—roads, public housing—provided little or no return on investment in the short run and were the worst kind to enter into during a period of severe adjustment in energy prices. In addition, Peru was, through the 1970s, a wild market for foreign firms offering totally financed turnkey projects worth billions of dollars, for ideas like irrigating deserts at a cost per hectare four times higher than the price of land in Iowa.

Therefore, only one of every four dollars lent to the Peruvian state by the commercial banks was invested, taking into consideration the need to generate foreign cash with which to repay. This lack of rationality was possible because the military government of the 1970s had been able to convince foreign bankers, at the time of the petrodollar glut, that the Amazon jungle was loaded with massive amounts of oil, which later proved not to be the case. The Peruvian government also convinced some American liberal academicians, including some World Bank technocrats, that they were performing social transformations that were necessary for the country's development. As a result, many of these analysts rather naively overlooked external and fiscal deficits, only later to be surprised when this nice country run by a progressive military making reforms declared it could not meet its debt.

The Effect of Capital Flight

Another odd circumstance in the case of Peru is the surprisingly small amount of capital flight that has taken place. Oscar Ugarteche, a distinguished economist from the Peruvian Marxist left, who is obviously not interested in defending the local bourgeoisie, has estimated, in a recent paper, an average yearly capital-flight figure of $129 million for the period 1971-75; he also estimated a capital inflow of $109 million for the 1976-81 period and $100 million of capital flight for 1982 and, again, in 1983.[4]

Morgan Guaranty Trust estimates that through the period 1976-86, Peru registered very little capital flight.[5] Its figure for the last year of that period indicated a net inflow of $400 million. The U.S. Treasury Department believes that, currently, Peruvians keep about $1.4 billion abroad,[6] much less, in comparison to its external debt or any other economic indicator, than Argentinians, Mexicans, or Venezuelans. My own estimates are somewhat higher, but not to the point where a return of assets currently held abroad could be considered a significant solution to Peru's problems.

Overwhelming Economic and Social Problems

Peru is moving backward. Twenty-five years ago, Peru exported three times more than South Korea; last year, it exported ten times less. Compared with its its five neighboring countries,* Peru was behind only Chile in GDP per capita in the early sixties; now, it is behind all but Bolivia.

* Since it won its independence, Peru has had nine military confrontations with the five nations with which it shares its borders, causing its defense expenditures to run high.

But poverty is not as much a factor in political instability as is frustration. In the past fifteen years, Peru has been growing at half the rate of the Latin American region as a whole. Its per capita income is the same as it was twenty years ago. These economic problems have not only affected the economy of the country, but have also undermined its political stability. There are no new pieces of pie to hand out to the increasing number of people. The competition for the existing shares has, therefore, become increasingly intense and violent.

Peru's foreign debt is probably the least important part of the current crisis. Even if the world were to forgive Peru that debt, the economy would still be facing the greatest crisis of this century, with yearly four- or five-digit inflation. The public-sector deficit for 1988 has been more than 10 percent of GDP in a country not fully aware, politically, that there is no more space for this spending spree.[7] The central bank has had, since July 1985, to increase nominal liquidity by more than 6,000 percent in order to finance the government deficit. Expansionary policies have, once more, failed in a Latin American economy. Rudiger Dornbusch, a professor of economics at MIT who was in Lima in mid-1987 at the invitation of the Peruvian government, concluded that, without urgent fiscal austerity measures, the Peruvian program was "poetry" that would require a "magician" to make it work. From such a firm neo-Keynesian, a statement of this nature should have canceled any optimistic expectations regarding the economy. For Peru, 1989 will be the worst year of the century, promising a severe recession (the GDP is expected to fall by more than 10 percent), hyperinflation, and no international reserves in an environment of rising social expectations and increasing violence and terrorism.

Emerging from this crisis will take time. Gross investment, which was over 20 percent of GDP during the 1950s and early 1960s with little external debt, has fallen to 12 percent of GDP. With such a low level of gross investment, it will be very difficult, in the coming years, for GDP to grow at a rate higher than that of the population (about 2.7 percent a year).

Which Way to Go?

Alan Garcia was right to give more importance to economic growth than to payment of external debt, but wrong in the way he has gone about it and wrong to employ the type of harsh political rhetoric he has when addressing the international community. On the other hand, the IMF and the international banking community have been clear in identifying the need for structural adjustment, but, as in the past, have been absolutely wrong in the means and particularly the timing recommended for achieving such difficult goals in a country as troubled as Peru.

Even if a coherent stabilization program were to be designed and applied in Peru, treatment of the debt issue—as in Bolivia and some Central American countries—could not be managed without a selective debt-relief program such as the one suggested by Jeffrey D. Sachs.[8] Given balance of payments projections, no matter what policies are followed, nations such as Peru cannot just "muddle through" this debt crisis. Authors like William Cline have explained in detail why debt relief could be harmful for restoring creditworthiness in the long run. I fully agree, but in the short run Peru will not survive without it.

For the region as a whole, debt relief should be considered not on the basis that the present situation cannot continue, but that it should not continue. The United States, as the predominant power in the hemisphere, must take bold and positive actions to alleviate the unnecessary costs that the debt burden imposes on countries throughout Latin America. Peruvians need to see some light at the end of the tunnel in order to put aside their preoccupation with—and stress and anxiety over—the debt problem. Only then will they be able to turn their attention to increasing productivity, growth, political stability, and their own standard of living.

Peru and the Future of Latin America

As has been explained, unpopular orthodox adjustments will be necessary if Peru is to put its house in order. There are a number of questions about Peru, its future, and how its efforts to come to grips with the present crisis affect the rest of Latin America. For example, Will Garcia accept a significant restructuring in his economic program? Must hyperinflation run wild before the government faces reality? Will the Garcia government increasingly try to find a scapegoat for its economic failure? Are any of these processes politically manageable without a breakdown of the entire Peruvian system of politics? What role should the international community play in the coming years? Has Peru any future at all? If Sendero Luminoso were to succeed in Peru, would it bring a Maoist-type revolution in Latin America? And if that is a possibility, how will other nations respond?

The situation is obviously a rich mine for international journalists and analysts. Michael Nacht has identified some social and political indicators for estimating the likelihood of change, not only of a government, but of an entire political and cultural system in a given country.[9] According to him, aside from economic performance—which, as has been explained before, could be dramatically disappointing in Peru, the following factors are critical:

- the ideology of the opposition
- the origins of the regime
- some basic social and demographic indicators
- corruption
- repression
- the possibility of catalytical events
- the attitude of foreign powers.

Ideology of the opposition. APRA is in the center of the Peruvian official political spectrum. Between it and the terrorists of Sendero Luminoso, a variety of radical and moderate-left groups have formed a United Left front whose main leader is Alfonso Barrantes, a Marxist former mayor of Lima who has the support of the Soviet-backed Peruvian Communist party. To the right of the APRA, the two organized parties that formed a government coalition during the previous administration of Fernando Belaunde have joined forces with an independent group led by Mario Vargas Llosa. What makes Barrantes the main leader of the United Left is not ideology but personal charisma. He could draw 10 percent more votes in the polls than any of his more ideological peers. His close friendship with Garcia, however, is one of the reasons why his opposition to the government is not seen as being clear and straightforward.

Vargas Llosa is willing to wage a more ideological opposition campaign, but first he has to convince his newfound colleagues to join him in taking such a stand. Until now, the major event that has galvanized these groups has been their opposition to the nationalization of the banks.

So the ideology of the opposition is not yet strong enough to affect Garcia's day-to-day decisions. It is more due to his own mistakes than to the emergence of new political messages that his popular support is falling apart.

At the extreme, Sendero's ideology may sound somewhat coherent, but only to the very desperate who have nothing to lose by getting involved in a bloody terrorist insurgency. Unfortunately, this is a group that is rapidly increasing in number.

Origins of the regime. Garcia's regime draws its legitimacy from being elected in a free election by a landslide. The economic crisis, however, has given birth to a number of rumors, including Garcia's threats to resign or to push for a declaration of a "state of emergency" that could be used as a pretext for postponing the 1990 elections and establishing a military-backed "emergency regime." My own opinion is that the most stable situation would develop if there were a democratic transition of powers to a center-right government in 1990, but Barrantes is still leading in the polls against both Vargas Llosa and Alva (with 29-26-11 percent as of October 1988). Freedom of the press—which the government has, up to now, duly respected—is critical for the coming confrontation of ideas. A triumph of the United Left in 1990—in search of a Salvador Allende-kind of government—or economic or social chaos during 1989, or the attempt of the government to frustrate the results, if not the 1990 election itself, could develop into a military coup, which two-thirds of the people are against. A sign of Peruvian political maturity is that the same people who disagree with Garcia's political performance want him to remain in office until free elections choose his successor.

Basic social and demographic indicators. Some of these indicators are unfavorable for political stability in Peru: urbanization has been enormous and concentrated in Lima, the capital; enrollment in universities has increased massively, more than the demand for professionals, and the poor quality of education easily leads students to frustration and dogmatism; life expectancy, average nutritional levels, and access to drinking water and medical services are about the lowest in the region, partly as a result of Peru's geography.

Corruption. A closed and controlled economy brings about an increase in corruption. No effort has been made, even in presidential circles, to keep wrongdoing under control and to maintain a clean record.

Repression. The massacre of alleged terrorists who took part in three prison revolts as a consequence of what appears to have been a "misunderstanding" of presidential orders has left those responsible as yet unpunished. Aside from this and continual incidents where peasants are killed in confrontations between the army and terrorists in the Ayacucho rural area, the birthplace of Sendero Luminoso, currently under military control and in a state of civil war, reports of Amnesty International regarding the Peruvian situation do not show a substantial increase in the level of repression. Given a terrorist group of the strength and beliefs of Sendero, any civilian government would feel compelled to call for some minimum of repression to ensure security.

Catalytic events. The future months could be full of potential catalytic events, including a coup, in Peru. Garcia has been so accustomed to exercising his own will that he is likely to take actions in order to avoid losing more popular support. There are increasing tensions between the president and APRA, the president and his cabinet; also between the executive, and Congress, and between both powers and the judiciary. Garcia, who has a wild imagination and a history of provoking confrontations, may still have some cards up his sleeve.

Attitude of foreign powers. Peru, in the middle of the west coast of South America, sharing borders with five other countries, figures in the geopolitical calculus of many foreign powers. The USSR may attempt to increase its influence in the country, but Gorbachev's regime does not seem to support revolution. Rather, it would more probably induce Barrantes to moderate his platform for the coming elections. On the other hand, events in Brazil, Chile, and Argentina are, over the next few years, likely to be a major consideration in determining the risk of military intervention.

This analysis based on Nacht's criteria can lead to a number of possible scenarios ranging from a democratic transfer of power in 1990 to a right-of-center government and president, most probably Vargas Llosa, in the midst of a four- to five-digit annual inflation rate to Lima replacing Beirut as a divided city, cut in pieces by a civil war. In that broad range of possibilities, one should not exclude many in-betweens: a Nicaraguan-type society, a repressive military coup, Garcia resigning or even changing course in order to introduce minor orthodox economic policies after a period of such expensive populism.

The question is what can be done, if anything, to ensure that the road Peru takes is the soundest for its future. The response is that many players will have to take active roles in seeing to it that all the right things happen. I will attempt in the following chapter to provide some recommendations for the roles foreigners should play in order to solve the Peruvian puzzle.

6 / Recommendations

It is obvious that little could be achieved without the government of Peru taking the initiative for putting its house in order. However, Peru's problems will persist unless the governments of the creditor nations, the multinational lending agencies, and the major international banks join together with the government of Peru to work out a means of alleviating the nation's crushing debt burden enough to allow new growth to take place. I believe that if each of these groups collaborates in a coherent solution, the path to a resumption of development can be found: the pieces of the Peruvian debt puzzle can be joined together to form a future agenda for a healthy, growing nation. The recommendations I am putting forth are addressed to each of the foreign groups that must take part in solving the puzzle:

To the OECD Governments, Especially the United States

All governments should be aware of the urgent need for a framework for supervising international financial markets. International banking needs supervision just as much as national banking, more than half a century ago, needed it. The governments of the industrialized nations must create the political conditions that will allow the banks to make the sacrifices that reality will, in any event, impose. In addition, the major industrialized nations at the GATT talks must understand that the only way to avoid banking troubles at home is to lower the barriers against developing-country exports.

By promoting a more comprehensive and flexible menu—which should include some forms of debt relief—the United States could become a firmer ally for the new democracies of Latin America rather than a financial adversary. This shift in attitude could give these governments the will, the incentive, and the political standing to go forward with true reform programs. Only then could the Latin American governments tell their people—as President Paz Estenssoro was able to do in Bolivia—that the reforms and economic sacrifices they were being asked to make were truly for their own benefit, and not for the sake of foreign banks.

The key, according to Jeffrey Sachs, could be to turn the banks' declines in the stock market into real relief for the debtor countries, while at the same time protecting the banks from any further declines.[1] For debtor countries willing to pursue adjustment programs under adequate supervision, an international agency such as the World Bank could purchase bank debt at the discount price. The purchase could, of course, be made with marketable bonds rather than cash. Then, the World Bank or other agency would reduce the debt burden to the discounted amount. In this way, the debt burden would be reduced to a level that the country could reasonably be expected to service.

The big question for Washington remains: Can bureaucracy transcend its usual shortsightedness to see the need for a creative, concerted write-down of at least some Third World debt before the majority of debtor nations turn toward unilateral debt repudiation? The odds that this will happen are not good; everyone involved is more likely to "muddle through."

Up to now, in its bilateral relations the U.S. government has been very cool and professional, acting with unusual tact and overcoming the impulse on the part of some to "teach Peru a lesson." Ambassador Alexander Watson has been doing a remarkable job in Lima. Although decisions regarding Peru's uncertain future belong exclusively to the Peruvian government, the overall approach of the U.S. government to the situation may become a critical factor in Peru's decisionmaking process. In the end, the industrialized nations must accept that what finally happens to Peru, the traditional center of South America from Spanish colonial days—its society, political structure, and economy—will have an effect on the rest of the region.

To the IMF and World Bank

History indicates the need for caution and limited objectives for multilateral agencies in helping the economies of Latin America to restore stability and growth. I agree fully with Jeffrey Sachs that:

> 1. Conditionality is unlikely to be very effective in coaxing governments to undertake unpopular policies, or in enabling them to overcome the problem of time consistency. The sanctions attached to conditionality are inherently too weak to provide much hope for strong

programs. This weakness seems to be inherent in the political and institutional role which the World Bank and the IMF are called upon to fill.

2. The overhang of debt greatly complicates the situation. In cases of extreme indebtedness, the debt itself might set up incentives that are adverse to significant adjustment or liberalization.

3. The historical experience with liberalization alone, and with stabilization alone, are not very encouraging. The difficulties of combining the two policy initiatives are formidable. The historical record suggests reasons for believing that inflation should first be brought under control, before any serious attempt is made to liberalize the economy.[2]

For these reasons, the international agencies should put greater stress on several factors when designing new programs. First, the Fund and the Bank should wait for member governments to take the lead in formulating stabilization programs rather than do battle with the member governments to force them to accept programs designed in Washington. Peru can serve as a clear example of how programs not fully supported by the government are inevitably condemned to failure. Second, the Fund and the Bank should stand back and encourage write-downs of private-sector debt for special cases like Peru, rather than attempting to bridge what is, obviously, an unclosable financial gap. The incentives for conditionality and liberalization are simply all wrong in the case of a country with a "hopeless" debt overhang such as Peru's. What is required is a sustained period of heavy investment in the export sector as well as of macroeconomic stability, both of which are difficult under conditions of financial crisis. A substantial "time out" from the crisis in the form of a reduction in the debt-service burden is a prerequisite to economic recovery. In addition, conditionality agreements require new rules of the game rather than one-time policy actions. For example, instead of insisting on a given devaluation figure, a conditionality agreement should require a move to real exchange rates; instead of a one-shot rise in public-sector prices, the agreement should describe a system for indexing them in real terms, and so forth. Also, some aspects of the development philosophy of these institutions, their underlying models of consumption and technology, should be questioned and, perhaps, revised in the light of experience.

Changes in these institutions should not be decided by the industrial countries alone. On the contrary, involving the debtors in designing the formulas could bring several benefits. Adjustment policies should use policy instruments more selectively and be more concerned about questions of equity. This is essential for the economic viability of Latin American democracies. The overall gains will be much greater if representatives of the debtor countries play a meaningful role in determining their future. The establishment of stabilization committees in each borrowing country, with an IMF and World Bank presence, would contribute to improving oversight of the adjustment process. The governments of the industrialized countries would be in a stronger position to sell these ideas if they took the form of an international agreement backed by other democratic states.

Finally, Structural Adjustment Loans (SALs) should have as their aim the development of new mechanisms for encouraging private-sector investment. Indeed, part of the new funds should be used for the joint financing of private-sector investments.

To the Commercial Banks

Bankers need little advice. Although the banks have been protesting the debtors' demands for the past six years, things have gone better for them than they had any right to expect. Most of the concessions they have made in their successive packages of rescheduling and "concerted" lending have preserved the net present value of the debtors' obligations. In that sense, the banks have yielded nothing, even though their problems were caused as much by their own profligacy as by some economic policies of the industrialized countries and the debtors' incompetence.

The international bankers did in fact allow themselves to become balance of payments lenders, forgetting their proper role as financiers of specific projects or enterprises. In their aggressive lending to certain countries, the bankers were often pursuing opportunities that were totally unconnected with the credit operation itself. Similarly aggressive salesmanship on the part of some exporters in the industrial West resulted in the bankrolling of white elephant projects and the conspicuous consumption that contributed little to the real economic development of countries such as Peru.

Creditors must assume responsibility for resolving the foreign debt problem. The present general practice has placed the burden almost entirely on the shoulders of the debtors. This cannot continue. If the creditors refuse to accept their share of the responsibility for the debtors' problems voluntarily, the international financial system will, sooner or later, be threatened by a collapse.

Could the banks afford these losses? Probably yes, since they have already been incurred in their stock market valuations and loan-loss reserves. Sachs has implied from his research that partial debt-relief could be to the benefit of both parties (Pareto-improving) by providing incentives to the debtor country to make needed adjustments. Of course, as William Cline has implied, the ideas I am endorsing would take the banks out of long-term financing for most Latin American states, but this is a business that the banks themselves are now eager to abandon, unless it is done as part of a cofinancing arrangement with multilateral institutions.

Private lenders should accept some kind of interest rate caps, lower spreads, and the conversion of a part of their credit into risk capital. When Citibank made significant provisions against Third World debt—prompting many other American and British banks to follow suit—it did so partly to prepare for an expanded program of debt-equity swaps.

Ideas like swaps or interest rate caps are ways of shifting risk from debtors to lenders, so it is hardly surprising that the lenders are generally unenthusiastic about them. But lenders should remember that when they reduce the risks to debtors, they also reduce the broader risks to the system, risks that they are all facing.

Currently, the greatest single danger of the debt situation is a sharp rise in interest rates. Unlike a change in oil prices, such a rise would hit all debtors simultaneously—and hard. Nothing is more likely to provoke a debtors' cartel and large-scale defaults. If, by capping interest rates and thereby accepting a larger measure of commercial risk, the banks can eliminate that danger, it seems a small price to pay.

* * *

Peru was already an old civilization when the Spanish arrived in the sixteenth century. However, a fratricidal war among the Incas was tearing the empire apart. A civil war also developed among the Spanish as soon as the booty of the conquest was divided. After three centuries of colonial rule, Peruvians gained indpendence through a war that lasted three years and left the Peruvian economy in shambles. Three decades after that, guano gave the republican state its first boom and the world financial centers the first indication of the inability of Peru to use credit properly. After a long war with Chile in the late nineteenth century, the Peruvian government defaulted on its own paper money.

Through all these dramatic events, as Jorge Basadre used to say, *"Peru kept on being Peru."* Indicators of economic depression, hyperinflation, and terrorist violence make this current crisis the worst in history. It is not only affecting the standard of living of the Peruvian masses and therefore the credibility of fragile democratic institutions, but also, as recent migration figures illustrate, creating a loss of faith in the country's future. The next several years are critical for the effort to reverse this trend. To achieve this, Peruvian leaders should understand hope as defined by the Argentine writer Jorge Luis Borges: "a terrible and secret duty."

Appendixes

Appendix 1

Peru: Basic Economic Indicators

	1970	1971	1972	1973	1974	1975
GDP Growth (%)	7.3	5.1	5.8	6.2	6.9	2.4
GDP per capita (US$)[a]	470	500	550	650	780	840
Internal Savings						
(% of GDP)	15.9	14.9	14.2	13.9	12.3	8.5
Gross Investment						
(% of GDP)	12.9	15.3	14.5	16.0	19.5	19.7
Public Investment						
(% of GDP)	4.5	4.6	4.9	5.5	8.2	8.3
Inflation						
Dec./Dec. (%)	5.7	7.5	4.2	13.8	19.1	24.0
Devaluation against US$						
Dec./Dec. (%)	0.0	0.0	0.0	0.0	0.0	16.3
Fiscal Income						
(% of GDP)	16.1	15.6	15.5	14.8	15.2	16.0
Public-Sector Deficit						
(% of GDP)	0.8	1.5	2.9	4.5	6.9	9.7
Exports, f.o.b.						
((US$ billions)	1.03	0.89	0.94	1.11	1.50	1.33
Imports, f.o.b.						
(US$ billions)	0.70	0.73	0.81	1.03	1.91	2.43
Current Account Balance						
(US$ millions)	185	(34)	(32)	(192)	(807)	(1,535)
(% of GDP)	3.0	- 0.5	- 0.4	- 2.1	- 7.0	- 11.3

Source: Felipe Ortiz de Zevallos and Guillermo Thornberry, *Hipoteca y Rescate* (Lima: Mosca Azul Editores and APOYO S.A., 1985).

a. Gross estimates due to exchange rate differences.

b. For nontraditional exports there was a "dirty" (covert) devaluation of 31 percent.

n.a.: Not available.

Appendix 1 (continued)

	1976	*1977*	*1978*	*1979*	*1980*	*1981*
GDP Growth (%)	3.3	- 0.3	- 1.8	4.3	2.9	3.1
GDP per capita (US$)[a]	880	785	654	824	995	1,136
Internal Savings (% of GDP)	10.3	8.9	12.9	21.0	17.1	13.5
Gross Investment (% of GDP)	17.7	14.8	14.4	14.3	17.7	22.2
Public Investment (% of GDP)	7.9	6.2	5.5	5.6	7.3	9.0
Inflation Dec./Dec. (%)	44.8	32.4	73.7	66.7	60.8	72.7
Devaluation against US$ Dec./Dec. (%)	52.7	81.2	55.5	28.1	35.8	47.7
Fiscal Income (% of GDP)	14.6	14.6	15.7	17.7	20.5	17.9
Public-Sector Deficit (% of GDP)	10.1	9.7	6.1	1.1	4.7	8.4
Exports, f.o.b. ((US$ billions)	1.34	1.73	1.97	3.68	3.92	3.25
Imports, f.o.b. (US$ billions)	2.02	2.15	1.67	1.95	3.09	3.80
Current Account Balance (US$ millions)	(1,072)	(783)	(164)	953	(102)	(1,729)
(% of GDP)	- 7.8	- 6.2	- 1.5	7.0	- 0.6	- 8.6

Appendix 1 (continued)

	1982	*1983*	*1984*	*1985*	*1986*	*1987*
GDP Growth (%)	0.9	- 12.0	4.7	1.9	8.5	6.9
GDP per capita (US$)[a]	1,116	864	882	733	1,004	1,347
Internal Savings						
(% of GDP)	14.9	11.6	14.5	14.5	8.9	n.a.
Gross Investment						
(% of GDP)	22.6	17.0	16.1	14.1	14.2	12.2
Public Investment						
(% of GDP)	10.3	10.3	9.5	7.3	6.1	5.0
Inflation						
Dec./Dec. (%)	72.9	125.1	111.5	158.3	62.9	114.5
Devaluation against US$						
Dec./Dec. (%)	90.7	135.5	132.7	168.1	0.0[b]	101.1
Fiscal Income						
(% of GDP)	17.5	14.2	16.2	17.9	15.3	11.3
Public-Sector Deficit						
(% of GDP)	9.3	12.1	7.2	4.4	7.9	10.9
Exports, f.o.b.						
((US$ billions)	3.29	3.02	3.15	2.98	2.53	2.6
Imports, f.o.b.						
(US$ billions)	3.72	2.72	2.14	1.81	2.60	3.0
Current Account Balance						
(US$ millions)	(1,609)	(871)	(221)	125	(1,055)	(1,317)
(% of GDP)	- 7.9	- 5.4	- 1.3	0.9	- 5.0	- 4.7

Appendix 2

Evolution of the Public Debt

Table A2.1
Public External Debt
Original Schedule of Payments by Source (US$ million)

	1983			1984			1985			1986		
	A	I	T	A	I	T	A	I	T	A	I	T
Government and Governmental Agencies (Paris Club)	194	97	291	172	95	267	129	99	228	143	91	234
Commercial Banks	335	285	620	617	355	972	288	266	554	506	179	685
Multilateral Organizations	44	47	91	72	75	147	76	86	162	120	126	246
Soviet Union and East Bloc	214	63	277	248	53	301	375	70	445	243	46	289
Private Suppliers	358	134	492	517	256	773	461	217	678	436	159	595
Total	1,145	626	1,771	1,626	834	2,460	1,329	738	2,067	1,448	601	2,049

Source: General Office of Public Credit—MEF.

Table A2.2
Evolution of the Public External Debt
(US$ million)

	1983	1984	1985	1986
1. Disbursements	2,554	1,720	859	430
2. Payments	1,751	1,160	816	523
Amortization	1,145	751	527	290
Interest	606	409	289	233
3. Net Cash Flow	803	560	43	(93)
4. Increments in Arrears	20	1,310	1,251	1,526
Amortization	–	885	802	1,158
Interest	20	425	449	368
5. Moratorium Coefficient (%) (4)÷(2+4)	1.1	53.0	60.5	74.5
6. Net Flow with No Moratorium	783	(750)	(1,208)	(1,619)
7. Accumulated Arrears	20	1,330	2,581	4,107
Amortization		885	1,687	2,845
Interest	20	445	894	1,262
8. Owed by 12/31 (I)	8,339	9,731	10,510	11,018
(II)		9,779	10,666	11,233
(III)		9,802	10,743	11,337

Note:
(I) With capitalization of interest.
(II) As (I), but including interest for arrears in capital amortization.
(III) As (II), but including interest on interest not paid.
Source: Drago Kisic, *De la Corresponsabilidad a la Moratoria: El Caso de la Deuda Externa Peruana 1970–1986,* July 1987. Edited by CEPEI.

Table A2.3
Public External Debt
Debt by Sources (US$ million)

	1982	1986
Government and Governmental Agencies (Paris Club)	1,194	1,924
Commercial Banks	2,069	3,351
Multilateral Organizations	949	1,473
Soviet Union and East Bloc	925	984
Private Suppliers	1,171	3,286
Total	6,908	11,018

Source: Official figures.

Table A2.4
Public External Debt with Government and Governmental Agencies (Paris Club)
1983–86 (US$ million)

	1983	1984	1985	1986
1. Disbursements	315	193	208	124
2. Payments	291	95	33	73
Amortization	194	71	13	45
Interest	97	24	20	28
3. Net Cash Flow	24	98	175	51
4. Increments in Arrears	–	182	195	161
Amortization	–	111	116	98
Interest	–	71	79	63
5. Moratorium Coefficient (%) (4)÷(2+4)	–	65.7	85.5	68.8
6. Net Flow with No Moratorium	24	(84)	(20)	(110)
7. Accumulated Arrears	–	182	377	538
Amortization	–	111	227	325
Interest	–	71	150	213
8. Owed by 12/31 (I)	1,215	1,508	1,782	1,924
(II)	–	1,514	1,802	1,953
(III)	–	1,518	1,815	1,969

Note:
(I) With capitalization of interest.
(II) As (I), but including interest for arrears in capital amortization.
(III) As (II), but including interest on interest not paid.
Source: Drago Kisic, *De la Corresponsabilidad a la Moratoria: El Caso de la Deuda Externa Peruana 1970–1986,* July 1987. Edited by CEPEI.

Table A2.5
Public External Debt with Commercial Banks
(US$ million)

	1983	1984	1985	1986
1. Disbursements	745	467	5	–
2. Payments	600	266	133	21
Amortization	335	95	8	–
Interest	265	171	125	21
3. Net Cash Flow	145	201	(128)	(21)
4. Increments in Arrears	20	706	421	664
Amortization	–	522	280	506
Interest	20	184	141	158
5. Moratorium Coefficient (%) (4)÷(2+4)	3.2	72.6	75.9	96.9
6. Net Flow with No Moratorium	125	(505)	(549)	(685)
7. Accumulated Arrears	20	726	1,147	1,811
Amortization	–	522	802	1,380
Interest	20	204	345	503
8. Owed by 12/31 (I)	2,499	3,055	3,193	3,351
(II)	–	3,084	3,277	3,452
(III)	–	3,034	3,338	3,493

Note:
(I) With capitalization of interest.
(II) As (I), but including interest for arrears in capital amortization.
(III) As (II), but including interest on interest not paid.
Source: Drago Kisic, *De la Corresponsabilidad a la Moratoria: El Caso de la Deuda Externa Peruana 1970–1986,* July 1987. Edited by CEPEI.

Table A2.6
Public External Debt with Multilateral Organizations
(US$ million)

	1983	1984	1985	1986
1. Disbursements	200	260	198	180
2. Payments	91	135	171	249
Amortization	44	60	85	121
Interest	47	75	86	128
3. Net Cash Flow	109	125	27	(69)
4. Increments in Arrears	–	12	(9)	(3)
Amortization	–	12	(9)	(3)
Interest	–	–	–	–
5. Moratorium Coefficient (%) (4)÷(2+4)	–	8.1	–	–
6. Net Flow with No Moratorium	109	113	36	(66)
7. Accumulated Arrears	–	12	3	–
Amortization	–	12	3	–
Interest	–	–	–	–
8. Owed by 12/31	1,105	1,305	1,146	1,473

Source: Drago Kisic, *De la Corresponsabilidad a la Moratoria: El Caso de la Deuda Externa Peruana 1970–1986,* July 1987. Edited by CEPEI.

Table A2.7
Public External Debt with the Soviet Union and East Bloc
(US$ million)

	1983	1984	1985	1986
1. Disbursements	364	218	241	29
2. Payments	277	276	264	108
Amortization	214	231	336	83
Interest	63	45	28	25
3. Net Cash Flow	87	(58)	(123)	(47)
4. Increments in Arrears	–	25	81	181
Amortization	–	17	39	160
Interest	–	8	42	21
5. Moratorium Coefficient (%) (4)÷(2+4)	–	8.3	18.2	62.6
6. Net Flow with No Moratorium	87	(83)	204	(228)
7. Accumulated Arrears	–	25	106	287
Amortization	–	17	56	216
Interest	–	8	50	71
8. Owed by 12/31 (I)	1,075	1,070	1,017	984
(II)	–	1,071	1,021	996
(III)	–	1,072	1,072	1,002

Note:
(I) With capitalization of interest.
(II) As (I), but including interest for arrears in capital amortization.
(III) As (II), but including interest on interest not paid.
Source: Drago Kisic, *De la Corresponsabilidad a la Moratoria: El Caso de la Deuda Externa Peruana 1970–1986,* July 1987. Edited by CEPEI.

Table A2.8
Public External Debt with Private Suppliers
(US$ million)

		1983	1984	1985	1986
1. Disbursements		930	582	207	97
2. Payments		492	388	115	72
Amortization		358	294	85	41
Interest		134	94	30	31
3. Net Cash Flow		438	194	92	25
4. Increments in Arrears		–	385	563	523
Amortization		–	223	376	395
Interest		–	162	187	128
5. Moratorium Coefficient (%) (4)÷(2+4)		–	49.8	83.0	87.9
6. Net Flow with No Moratorium		438	(191)	(471)	(498)
7. Accumulated Arrears		–	385	948	1,471
Amortization		–	223	599	994
Interest		–	162	349	477
8. Owed by 12/31	(I)	2,343	2,793	3,102	3,286
	(II)	–	2,805	3,148	3,362
	(III)	–	2,814	3,178	3,402

Note:
(I) With capitalization of interest.
(II) As (I), but including interest for arrears in capital amortization.
(III) As (II), but including interest on interest not paid.
Source: Drago Kisic , *De la Corresponsabilidad a la Moratoria: El Caso de la Deuda Externa Peruana 1970–1986,* July 1987. Edited by CEPEI.

Table A2.9
Private-Sector Medium- and Long-Term Debt
(US$ million)

	1980	1981	1982	1983	1984	1985	1986
1. Disbursements	180	295	378	132	100	44	35
2. Payments	226	284	409	398	385	291	133
Amortization	116	160	221	217	214	168	73
Interest	110	124	188	181	171	123	60
3. Net Cash Flow	- 46	11	- 31	- 265	- 285	- 247	- 98
4. Increments in Arrears	–	–	–	–	–	–	65
Amortization	–	–	–	–	–	–	33
Interest	–	–	–	–	–	–	32
5. Moratorium Coefficient (%) (4)÷(2+4)	0	0	0	0	0	0	32.8
6. Net Flow with No Moratorium	- 46	11	- 31	- 265	- 285	- 247	- 163
7. Owed by 12/31	1,372	1,507	1,664	1,580	1,466	1,342	1,304
8. Implicit Interest Rate		8.6	11.9	11.2	11.2	9.0	6.9

Source: Drago Kisic, *De la Corresponsabilidad a la Moratoria: El Caso de la Deuda Externa Peruana 1970–1986*, July 1987. Edited by CEPEI.

Table A2.10
Central Bank Use of IMF Credit
as of May 31, 1987 (US$ million)

Compensatory Financing Facility	307
Credit Tranche	118
Extended Facilities	341
Total	766

Source: International Monetary Fund.

Table A2.11
Long-Term Debt of the Central Reserve Bank
(US$ million)

	1983	1984	1985	1986
1. Owed by 12/31	1,088	862	825	781
IMF	698	699	702	716
Fondo Andino de Reservas	195	163	98	33
Others	195	–	25	32
2. Disbursements	566	131	–	–
3. Payments	228	411	179	146
Amortization	147	313	114	115
Interest [a]	81	98	65	31
4. Increments in Arrears [b]	–	–	55	161
Amortization	–	–	43	130
Interest	–	–	12	31
5. Interest Rate [b]	9.0	10.0	7.8	7.7
6. Net Cash Flow	338	(280)	(179)	(146)
7. Moratorium Coefficient	0	0	23.5	52.5

a. All correspond to the International Monetary Fund.
b. Estimated.
Note: Variations in exchange rates generate some differences among sources.

Table A2.12
Short-Term Public and Private Debt
(US$ million)

	1983	1984	1985	1986
1. External Short-Term Debt as of 12/31	1,513	1,330	1,117	1,295
2. Amount Withheld	962	800	800	800
3. Effective Short-Term Debt	551	530	317	495
4. Changes in Effective Debt	(548)	(21)	(213)	178
5. Interest Paid	223	13	10	8
6. Net Cash Flow	(771)	(365)	(335)	(77)

Source: Official figures.

Appendix 3

Comparing Peru and Her Neighbors

Comparing Peru to her Latin American neighbors is a cheerless enterprise. The critical nature of the Peruvian situation can only be compared to that of Bolivia and some Central American countries. The "muddling through" process for solving the debt problem, which has yet to prove its effectiveness for Mexico, Brazil, Argentina, or Venezuela, would probably not suffice for Peru. A combination of all the concessions given to any of the debtor countries would not allow Peru to meet the normal service of its foreign debt. Moreover, arrears, even to multilateral organizations, are accumulating. Peru needs to be treated as a special case. The adjustment program that is needed should take into consideration not only the income level of the population but the effects of the adjustment program on its distribution to be successful. The Peruvian GDP, one of the lowest in the region, has fallen the most in Latin America since 1970 (see Table A-3.1). Social indicators—life expectancy, infant mortality, and the percentage of the population with access to drinking water—are also among the worst in the region.

Table A-3.1
GDP Per Capita

Countries	*GDP 1983/ GDP 1970*
Argentina	0.94
Bolivia	0.93
Brazil	1.62
Chile	0.93
Colombia	1.34
Ecuador	1.64
Mexico	1.31
Peru	0.90
Dominican Republic	1.55
Uruguay	1.12
Venezuela	0.93

Source: CEPAL.

Peru has also had, over the past twenty five years, one of the largest relative reductions in the rate of gross investment among all the medium- and large-size countries of the region (see Table A-3.2).

Table A-3.2
Change in the Coefficients of Gross Investment
(As percentage of GDP)

Countries	*(1)* *Average* *1960-1966*	*(2)* *Average* *1974-1980*	*(2)÷(1)*
Argentina	19.6	24.9	1.27
Brazil	24.4	26.5	1.09
Chile	14.5	16.9	1.17
Colombia	17.6	18.6	1.06
Ecuador	13.6	25.6	1.88
Mexico	19.8	24.2	1.22
Peru	22.9	16.8	0.73
Uruguay	13.9	15.1	1.09
Venezuela	21.5	32.8	1.53

Source: IMF.

One explanation for this development is the crowding out of the Peruvian private sector during the seventies. As shown in Table A-3.3, the growth rate of Peru's public sector was the highest in the region, which is why only 10 percent of the total Peruvian debt belongs to the private sector, a much lower percentage than in the region as a whole.

Table A-3.3
Public-Sector Growth
(Percentages)

	Public Sector Expenditures/GDP	
Country	*1970*	*1982*
Argentina	33	35
Brazil	38	32
Chile	41	36
Colombia	26	30
Mexico	21	48
Peru	25	57
Venezuela	32	66

Source: IDB.

Since the expansion of the public sector, and indebtedness, was the action of a military government in a country that shares borders with five others and has a long coastline, it is not surprising that in 1982, among all Latin American countries, only Argentina, also under a military regime, spent relatively more than Peru for defense.

Table A-3.4
Defense Expenditures 1982

Countries	*Defense/Central Government (percent)*
Argentina	35.0
Brazil	6.5
Chile	24.5
Colombia	15.5
Ecuador	15.0
Mexico	6.0
Peru	34.6
Uruguay	15.0
Venezuela	11.7

Source: CEPAL.

Last but not least, between 1981 and 1984, Peru was the Latin American country that suffered the most from variations in world commodity prices (see Table A-3.5).

Table A-3.5
Variations in Terms of Trade

Countries	*Variations 1981/1984*
Argentina	- 12.6
Bolivia	- 0.6
Brazil	- 12.5
Chile	- 28.0
Colombia	- 3.9
Ecuador	- 21.3
Mexico	- 26.8
Peru	- 37.1
Dominican Republic	- 19.8
Uruguay	- 8.4
Venezuela	- 8.0

Source: CEPAL.

Notes

Chapter 1

1. "Peru Background Information," a private memorandum prepared by Merrill Lynch Pierce Fenner & Smith Inc., September 1982.

2. Anatole Kaletsky, *The Costs of Default* (New York: Priority Press Publications, 1985).

3. The information for this and the following sections has been taken from four basic sources:

- Oscar Ugarteche, *El Estado Deudor* (Lima: Instituto de Estudios Peruanos, 1986).
- Thomas Scheetz, *Peru and the International Monetary Fund* (Pittsburgh: University of Pittsburgh Press, 1986).
- David Scott Palmer, "Peru: The Authoritarian Legacy," in *Latin American Politics and Development,* ed. Howard J. Wiarda and Harvey F. Kline (Boulder, Colo.: Westview Press, 1985).
- Jonathan Hartlyn and Samuel A. Morley, eds., *Latin American Political Economy: Financial Crisis and Political Changes* (Boulder, Colo.: Westview Press, 1986).

4. Mentioned in John Gunther, *Inside Latin America* (1941; reprint, Westport, Conn.: Greenwood Press, 1975).

5. Ibid.

6. James C. Carey, *Peru and the United States, 1900–1962* (Notre Dame, Ind.: University of Notre Dame Press, 1964).

7. Jose Luis Bustamante Rivero, *Tres Anos de Lucha por la Democracia en el Peru* (Buenos Aires: Bartolome U. Chefino, 1949).

8. Peru has had, between 1954 and 1980, nineteen standby (or extended fund facility) programs, more than any other country in Latin America.

9. Scheetz, *Peru and the International Monetary Fund.*

10. "A Program for the Industrial and Regional Development of Peru," Cambridge, Mass., Arthur D. Little Inc., 1960.

Chapter 2

1. Pedro-Pablo Kuczynski, *Peruvian Democracy under Economic Stress: An Account of the Belaunde Administration, 1963-1968* (Princeton, N.J.: Princeton University Press, 1977).

2. Hartlyn and Morley, *Latin American Political Economy.*

3. Barbara Stallings, "International Capitalism and the Peruvian Military Government, 1968–1978," Latin American Program at the Wilson Center working paper no. 20, Washington, D.C., 1978.

4. Scheetz, *Peru and the International Monetary Fund.*

5. "Desarrollar la Guerra Popular Sirviendo a la Revolucion Mundial," a Shining Path document signed in August 1986.

6. This hopeful appraisal of the Peruvian economy prevailed in 1966, 1974, and 1981, when delegates from aid organizations of the main European countries, together with those of the U.S. Treasury, the Agency for International Development, and the International Monetary Fund, convened in Paris under the auspices of the World Bank to decide on a coordinated aid package for Peru.

7. *Anatomia de un Fracaso Economico 1968-1978* (Lima: Centro de Investigacion de la Universidad del Pacifico, July 1979).

Chapter 3

1. Wiarda and Kline, *Latin American Politics and Development.*

2. *Victor Raul Haya de la Torre, Impresiones de la Inglaterra Imperialista y de la Rusia Sovietica* (Buenos Aires: Editorial Claridad, 1933).

3. Luis Rodriguez Vildozola, Carlos Manuel Cox, and Andres Townsend Escurra, eds., *El Plan de Accion. Pensamiento Politico de Haya de la Torre,* vol. 4 (Lima: Ediciones Pueblo, 1961).

4. A private document belonging to the author.

Chapter 4

1. *The Economist,* August 8, 1987.

Chapter 5

1. *The Economist,* June 27, 1987.

2. Andres Bianchi, Robert Devlen, and Joseph Ramos, "The Adjustment Process in Latin America, 1981-1986," in *Growth-Oriented Adjustment Programs: Proceedings of an IMF-World Bank Seminar,* ed. Vittorio Corbo, Morris Goldstein, and Mohsin Khan (Washington, D.C.: International Monetary Fund and World Bank, 1987).

3. Carol Wise, "Economia Politica del Peru: Rechazo a la Receta Ortodoxa," Instituto de Estudios Peruanos working paper no. 15, Lima, p. 38.

4. Oscar Ugarteche,"The Political Economy of International Default: The Cases of Peru and Bolivia," 48th Pugwash Symposium on Foreign Debts and International Stability, Lima, February 1987.

5. Editions of March 1986 and June/July 1987.

6. U.S. Treasury Bulletin and IMF International Financial Statistics.

7. For more information on the subject, see Felipe Ortiz de Zevallos, "Bank Nationalization Signals End of Peru's Spending Spree," *The Wall Street Journal,* August 14, 1987.

8. Jeffrey D. Sachs "A New Approach to Managing the Debt Crisis," *Columbia Journal of World Business* 21, no. 3 (Fall 1986).

9. Michael Nacht, "International Change and Regime Stability," London, International Institute for Strategic Studies, Adelphi Papers, no. 166.

10. APOYO S.A. is a publishing and consulting firm of which the author is founder and CEO. All the results presented in this paper correspond to surveys of 600 people in Lima. For a confidence level of 95 percent, they have a margin of error of $\pm$ 4 percent.

Chapter 6

1. Jeffrey D. Sachs, "It's the Right Time to Offer Real Relief," *The New York Times,* August 9, 1987.

2. Jeffrey D. Sachs, "Conditionality and the Debt Crisis: Some Thoughts for the World Bank," Cambridge, Mass., Harvard University, January 1986.

Index